THE ORDEAL OF
COEXISTENCE

THE GUSTAV POLLAK LECTURES
AT HARVARD UNIVERSITY

1962

THE ORDEAL OF
COEXISTENCE

BY WILLY BRANDT

HARVARD UNIVERSITY PRESS

CAMBRIDGE, MASSACHUSETTS · 1963

Library of Congress Catalog Card Number 63-15113
Printed in the United States of America

PREFACE

ON October 2 and 3, 1962, I had the pleasure and honor of delivering two lectures about questions of coexistence at Harvard University as part of the Gustav Pollak Lectures under the auspices of the Graduate School of Public Administration. Questions of coexistence are especially important in the life of my city of Berlin and for the future of my country. I was able to speak frankly at this lively center of political thought and, like many Europeans before me, I was made to feel very much at home. For this I wish to express my thanks.

The two lectures I delivered on that occasion have remained unchanged in substance here, although the recent Cuban crisis and other subsequent developments might have suggested that I bring up to date this or that section. The far-reaching effects of the Cuban crisis did not make necessary any changes in the ideas I developed at Harvard in the first week of October 1962. However, some additions and notes of explanation have been incorporated into the text, including long passages that had been left out in the original delivery because of the pressure of time. In a few places the connection with later events has been marked by a footnote. In this published form, the two original lectures have also been augmented by a third section concerning the German problem in the perspective of coexistence. This section was edited after the Cuban crisis.

I wish to thank those who have given me many valuable suggestions and comments as well as those who helped in preparation of the manuscript.

Willy Brandt

Berlin
December 1962

CONTENTS

THE concept of coexistence has gained currency as an expression of Communist propaganda and policy, constantly used, and abused, by the Soviets. It has met acceptance, even assent, throughout the world, especially in the uncommitted countries—which are so vastly important today.

Soviet propaganda has frequently given the impression that their offer of coexistence is tantamount to a policy of peace. Whoever rejects coexistence becomes suspect; he may be "against peace." The feeling is created that only one side has offered peaceful coexistence: the Soviets. The West, on the other hand, has incurred the stigma of negativism. This equating of Soviet-style coexistence with the concept of world peace beclouds the perils of the Soviet threat and weakens resistance against the Soviet thrust toward world supremacy.

Consciously or unconsciously, we are in danger of succumbing to another, no less invidious, suggestion: we are suspicious of the mere word "coexistence" because it is constantly bandied about by the Soviets. In this we forget a number of things. Coexistence is neither an invention of the Soviets nor their monopoly. On the contrary, coexistence is really suited to be one of democracy's own basic ideas; it belongs logically to the democratic principles of human dignity, tolerance, the right of self-determination, and national independence.

What then is *our* idea of coexistence? Applied in general terms, the word means that individuals, groups, and nations of different convictions and habits are living together without resorting to violence. In that sense coexistence is a fundamental law that affects many areas of human existence.

It follows that peaceful political coexistence would be more than a meaningless, or even hostile, proximity. In the literal sense it means living *with* each other. This coexistence with one another is based on mutual tolerance and a proper respect for the special characteristics and attitudes of others. So conceived, coexistence is the very essence of civilized conduct among nations in history. It is the only possible and reasonable way for the peoples to live together. Today, moreover, it has become a prerequisite condition for the continued progress of mankind.

According to this definition, coexistence is not confined in its application only to that portion of international relations which we call, in oversimplification, the East-West conflict. To our way of thinking it is a far wider concept; indeed, it is the only basis we have today for solving the urgent problems and conflicts that beset a world in which the industrial revolution has become a worldwide process, and in which developing countries must be integrated into the society of nations.

The tensions which threaten to tear our world asunder are probably graver than at any time in history—compounded as they are by the peril of total self-annihilation, for which the technical means now exist. Coexistence, therefore, becomes a question of mankind's very existence. In the real sense of the word, coexistence is not a mere alternative, but our only chance for survival.

In daily life coexistence means for us a state of affairs where opponents live together without the thunder of armor. In the longer view coexistence is for us the chance to prevail over Communist threats of violence.

In Berlin, the city I represent at the present time, the division of the world has become so stark that it can be photographed. Here we can see who is really both willing to coexist and capable of doing so. That is the reason why I will here first deal with the effects of the East-West conflict on Berlin. This is where, in the years since 1945, coexistence has been a living experience.

2

Until August 1961 Berlin had been a good example of peaceful competition. Communist East and democratic West faced each other across the street. Everyone could see for himself how the Western way of life compared with the Communist system.

Berlin was an open city, a cultural intersection, a place

where people and minds met, in spite of different cur-
rencies, different administrations, and political systems
which were diametrically opposed. For most Berliners,
the border between the eastern and western sectors was
a demarcation line which did not seriously inhibit their
movements. This line was crossed and recrossed at least
half a million times each day. More than 60,000 Berliners
lived in the eastern sector and worked in the western.
West Berlin sold more than ten million tickets each year
for concerts, plays, movies, exhibitions, and sports events
to the people in the eastern sector of Berlin and in the
surrounding area of the Soviet occupied zone of Germany.

In spite of the administrative division of the city de-
creed in 1948, in a very important sense Berlin continued
to be one cohesive community. Although certain Communist restrictions did exist, under the protective roof of
the four-power statute at least most citizens of Berlin
could move around freely. Thus until August 13, 1961,
Berlin was an arena of competitive coexistence in the
political, economic, and ideological fields—not however
in military matters. By agreement of the three Western
powers and the Soviet Union, the military factor was
kept firmly frozen and under control. Every day in
Berlin anybody could gain a firsthand impression of the
two systems, and ours was found superior.

The contest in the political, economic, and ideological
field was lost by Walter Ulbricht and his supporters.
Political pressures and economic difficulties caused 3.7
million inhabitants of the so-called German Democratic

Republic to flee to the West. Truly and unmistakably, people "voted with their feet." More than half of these refugees were younger than 25 years old. The youth which the Communists had hoped to win over and educate for their cause were deciding for the West.

It was this constant drain—the specter of an industry without workers, a party without members, a regime without a people—for which Ulbricht knew no other remedy but to put up the Wall. The Wall has cut my city in half. The Wall has separated one out of every two families in Berlin. It separates father from son, mother from daughter, bridegroom from bride.

This wall of shame has now become so massive and so high that only a few, risking their lives, can surmount it. We know of human tragedies which defy description. And yet, we know only of a small part of the human tragedies which occur day and night behind the Wall, behind the barbed wire.

The Soviets, reacting to the mass escape from their German protectorate, gave their consent to Ulbricht's Wall; they approved Ulbricht's order to shoot down those who attempt to cross it. Human beings who simply want to get to their friends or relatives in the other part of their city have become moving targets. And there is no indication that this appalling inhumanity will cease in the near future.

With this on our minds, it gives me no satisfaction to be able to state that Berlin has demonstrated convincingly that genuine coexistence does mean competition and that it is a contest which Communism must lose. At least in our part of the world Khrushchev has been taught the lesson that the Soviet paradise can only thrive behind prison walls. But it has also been demonstrated that under the pressure of defeat the Soviets resort to force; and this increases the danger of a military conflict.

We in West Berlin have mastered the problems with which the crisis of the Wall confronted us in 1961. Our economy continues to thrive and the morale of the population has held firm because we know that the welfare of the city outweighs all other considerations—even our hatred of the Wall.

Berlin has now lived for four years with the crisis that began with the Soviet ultimatum. The Wall is the product of these four years. It is the most brutal method imaginable for preventing the flood of refugees, but it is also the most convincing propaganda against Communism there has been since 1917. Khrushchev can draw no benefit at all from the Wall. The balance of the past four years still adds up to a loss for him. In Berlin we could hold out another four years, go on building up our city, and then take another accounting. The balance for Khrushchev would be even more negative than it is now. That is why I believe that conversations with the Soviets about Berlin can be meaningful. Without a war there is nothing in Berlin that Khrushchev can win any longer. The only question is whether he knows it.

All Berliners are grateful for the help extended to us by our friends. Without the Allies' iron guarantees, a free Berlin would no longer exist. We are aware of the significance of the fact that the United States has tied its fate to that of West Berlin. And there is no need for continued reassurances that this commitment has not been altered. If such pledges are needed at all, it is Khrushchev who should be made aware of them. For there is hardly any doubt that he will go precisely as far as he dares without risking a major war—and Berlin is certainly not the only place where that applies.

The question "Why die for Berlin?" is put incorrectly. At least those in the West must not ask that question unless we want to slip into the position of being blackmailed. Since the discovery of the atom bomb, at the very latest, it has become impossible to weigh the advantages or disadvantages of making war on a scale which measures whether two, five, or fifty million people would at first be involved.

Here a principle is at stake; it is a question of what the West stands for and how firmly. The East must also be asked if Moscow wants to go to war for its Berlin objectives. If the answer to that question is yes then Moscow will get its war; neither the cowardly nor the courageous among us could deter the Kremlin from starting the war it wants.

Only if we take a firm stand—especially in Berlin—can we avoid a major conflict. I do believe that it is in the interest of the Soviet Union to prevent a major war.

As I suggested before, the events of August 13, 1961, have changed the very character of my city. Berliners have to live with the Wall. It is not, of course, an easy matter to do that. The unmistakable bitterness of the people of Berlin shows that they have learned from the

Hitler years: never again will they passively accept in-
justice. Yet their rightful indignation is curbed by a
proper desire to maintain peace. The situation forces
Berliners to control their emotions, to think and act
reasonably. I have cautioned my fellow citizens never to
let their hearts overrule the verdict of their heads. But
they cannot permanently live without some idea of what
the future will bring. The present state of suspension and
uncertainty must be transformed into a reasonable interim settlement which promises a certain degree of
stability without, at the same time, obliterating Berlin's
real purport, namely to be a capital city.

Naturally, it is of no small value that more than two
million people in Berlin are able to live in freedom and in
comparative prosperity. Decisive, however, is whether
the Berliners and the West Germans, whom we want to
come to Berlin, believe in the future of the city. That is
just as important to Berlin's further development as is
the continued presence of the Western troops. Berlin
is not only a metropolitan city in Germany. It must
become the German capital city once again or it will
not have fulfilled its purpose.

It is precisely in Berlin, where the division of the
world has literally been cemented in stone, and where
the Soviet policy of coexistence is exposed in its naked
reality, that one must insist that coexistence cannot be a
synonym for maintenance of the status quo.

When the Berlin crisis began four years ago, Khrushchev had higher stakes in mind than merely to win, or
undermine, West Berlin. It was, and still is, his para-

mount aim to obtain official Western consent for the partition of Europe.

Six years ago, speaking at Harvard, Hugh Gaitskell said that he considered the permanent division of Europe one of the main reasons for Khrushchev's espousal of "peaceful coexistence" as a doctrine of Soviet foreign policy. Indeed, the Western seal of approval affixed to the map of a divided Europe should lend stability to his Eastern European realm.

However, Khrushchev also pursues offensive objectives in the Berlin crisis; by getting the West to consent to the partition of Germany, he would like to drive a wedge between West Germany and her allies; he wants to pry her loose from the Western community and thus undermine and, if possible, break up our alliance. By manipulating the lever of the Berlin crisis, he hopes to bring about Western withdrawal from Berlin, thus destroying confidence in any guarantee furnished by the United States anywhere in the world. That would pose an immediate threat to the national security of the United States itself.

The uprising in the Soviet zone of Germany in 1953 and the Hungarian revolution in 1956 have taught us that nonintervention by the West does little to placate Khrushchev. Although Western restraint, based on a reluctance to imperil world peace, is something he can depend upon, that has not been sufficient. For in the vast realm between Vladivostok and the Elbe there is still the open wound of dismembered Germany; and through Berlin the Soviet bloc was being drained of its strength.

For me, no experience of 1961 was more decisive than the realization that though, objectively speaking, we have won a victory in Berlin, the price has had to be paid by those who are our best friends, and for whom we have felt a devoted responsibility for so many years, namely, the people on the other side of the Wall, and especially the families on both sides of the Wall that have been torn asunder. It was a defeat for the Soviets, but for us it was a costly and bitter victory which we can never really enjoy.

The West can never be permanently reconciled to the Berlin Wall. A solution to the German question, which can only be based on the right of self-determination, must be kept on the agenda. But the question remains embedded in the worldwide East-West conflict, and therefore we cannot expect a solution overnight. We must continue to work for a modus vivendi in Berlin without, however, losing sight of the bigger problems. Thus far, it has not been possible to reach a settlement limited to any of the issues involving Berlin.

Meanwhile, more vigorous action can and should be taken on another plane. The Wall is an object lesson to the world, an affront to basic human rights. An offensive in the name of humanity could serve: (1) to compel the Soviet Union and its retinue to participate in an international debate about coexistence with the example of Berlin as the specific issue; and (2) to press stubbornly and without illusion for all possible alleviations of the suffering caused by the Wall. At least some of the most inhuman consequences of the Wall can be counteracted.

The situation of my city forces me daily to reflect on how we can tie in our long-term planning with the reality of today, how we can maintain our positions and win the future.

3

Let us say it once again: in Berlin Communism has been unable to stand the test of coexistence in its proper meaning. Communism has thus given proof that its concept of coexistence cannot be reconciled with that of true coexistence such as the world, if it is to survive, is in need of today. Can we therefore consider the Soviet demands for coexistence to be nothing more than a mere tactical device of Soviet policy at the moment?

It would be wrong to say so, because we know that the theory of coexistence has become an important and inseparable part of the political armory of Communism. We know also that Soviet policy as a rule needs urgently the crutches which Communist theory offers. Therefore, we must not make the mistake of belittling or of simply ignoring the Communist theory of coexistence as mere propaganda. If this Soviet doctrine were only propaganda, the intense ideological conflict between Moscow and Peiping would be meaningless.

If we want to understand Soviet policy properly and base our political calculations upon sound evaluations, then we must attempt to understand Soviet reasoning behind such policy.

The difference between the Communist doctrine of coexistence and our conception of coexistence reflects

our altogether different understanding of the nature of
the conflict that divides us. According to their doctrine,
the present world conflict is the irreconcilable struggle
between the two opposing camps, that of "capitalism"
and that of "socialism." In their view, the future belongs
only to those who are working for what they consider
to be socialism. The other camp is irrevocably condemned to perish. It is the historic duty of Communists
to hasten this historically necessary process. The essence
of the process is the so-called class struggle, which can
assume various forms, including a revolutionary war
which would, inevitably, be a just one. So-called "just
wars of liberation" merit support by the Communist
camp up to the point where they might get out of
control.

However, fearing the risk of atomic annihilation, the
Soviet Union today seeks to avoid a world war. It now
considers itself strong enough to force the capitalist
world to its knees by using primarily nonmilitary means:
"peaceful competitive coexistence." By this means, it is
expected, the superiority of the Communist system shall
be proved. Khrushchev himself has said it often enough:
today this kind of coexistence offers the best chances
for a successful prosecution of the international class
struggle. He calls this coexistence "peaceful" but really
it is still intended to be aggressive. Walls are erected
against a successful competitor and limited military actions are still considered appropriate.

With a charm that is uniquely his own and without
any equivocation, Khrushchev has stated that he will

bury us. And he appears to feel provoked when we seem reluctant to march along his own road of coexistence to the cemetery which he has prepared for us.

The Soviet formula for coexistence cannot be reconciled with our own concept of true coexistence. This is because, in the last analysis, he who equates coexistence with a guerrilla war rejects any form of cooperation that is stable and confident. As far as the Communists are concerned, to tolerate any other system is a heresy and a betrayal of the "true gospel." They scorn the very idea of "ideological coexistence" which, they say, would inevitably result in a softening of the "class struggle" in the international arena. The Communist camp, they argue, would thus lose its power of resistance when facing the West and it would succumb to revisionist tendencies.

The interests of the Soviet leadership are clear. Their theories are false. There is no inevitable conflict between states of different social and economic systems.

Within the Western and the neutral world there are many economic shadings ranging from old-school capitalism to variants of socialistic planned economy; yet these differences are not a source of tensions which threaten the peace. On the other hand, the Soviet Union is wrestling with certain reforms within an industrial society that is not free. No international conflicts are going to spring out of that process either. Beyond that, we find that the West is on fairly good terms with Communist Yugoslavia, and even Gomulka's Poland can count on a certain understanding in the West, even though in matters of foreign policy it scarcely has another choice but that of following the Soviet line.

The social and economic structures of different systems are not a cause for serious international conflicts. The real causes of the worldwide conflict are to be found in the polarization of power and in the claim to world supremacy raised by the Communist power centers, Moscow and Peiping, which seek to subjugate and reshape the world according to a rigid doctrine.

4

The way the Soviet leadership sees it, peaceful coexistence does not imply mutual toleration; Soviet coexistence is thus not coexistence in its proper meaning—not really peaceful but, on the contrary, militant.

Khrushchev and his ideologists have not even forsworn the classic Communist theory of "just" wars. The language of their diplomatic notes is still, as a rule, very bellicose. Actually, there is but a single concession wrapped up in their slogan of peaceful coexistence: although they threaten us with nuclear missiles, they would prefer not to launch them.

Peaceful coexistence Soviet style means the militant pursuit of Soviet aims—but with sufficient limitation and control of military methods to prevent them from becoming "independent" or growing on their own.

Lenin, Stalin, and Khrushchev have all sought to avoid becoming entangled in major wars. Even at the time when, under Lenin and Stalin, the Soviets were still convinced of the inevitability of wars, it was the paramount aim of their strategy to ensure the survival of the Soviet Union as an island "encircled" by the hostile ocean of capitalism.

Wherever possible, they added fuel to the fires of conflict between their enemies. They hoped in this way to prevent a worldwide anti-Soviet coalition. The prime example of this policy, we must never forget, was the Hitler-Stalin pact.

Until very recently the Soviets still believed that a military conflict was inevitable. However, they did think that they would be able to limit the risk to such an extent that the Soviet Union would remain unimpaired, with its continuous growth insured. This maneuvering was at the bottom of the earlier Soviet concept of coexistence —whether they called it by that or any other name.

Even as late as 1955–56, the slogan of "peaceful coexistence" was just one tactical device among many. Today it plays a far more important, indeed, a vital role; it has been elevated to the realm of grand strategy in the field of Soviet foreign policy; it has become part and parcel of the routine doctrine that every good Communist is expected to believe.

It remained for Khrushchev, the political pragmatist, to embellish coexistence with the trappings of ideological theory. His theory of coexistence is both propaganda and reality, and in each respect it is a two-pronged weapon. Significantly, the Soviets acknowledge and seek to banish the threat of thermonuclear annihilation. But Khrushchev has also developed "peaceful coexistence" into a strategic weapon in his offensive against the West. It has

become the Soviets' new device in their drive to para-
lyze and, finally, to conquer the non-Communist world
with every means suited to that purpose, short of a major
war.

In Khrushchev's mind peaceful coexistence is not the
search for ways to ensure permanent stability. It is a
basic tenet of Soviet ideology that the inexorable course
of history will vindicate Communism. Peaceful coexistence is expected to hasten that process. It is not even
a pause in their uninterrupted struggle, but merely
another possibility of enlarging their realm and their
sphere of influence without incurring the risk of nuclear
war. This is the practice of Soviet policy which has
taught the world a lesson from which we all should have
profited by now. It is their strategy to soften our resistance by maintaining a *precarious* peace—which means
keeping dangerous tensions alive.

At any moment that suits their convenience, the peace
is interrupted by plotted emergencies. Each of the points
of friction throughout the world waxes hot and cold on
signals from the Kremlin switchboard and in accord
with a strategic interest in making certain that international political tensions do not sink below a certain
critical level.

After World War II, from Stalin to Khrushchev, the
Soviet Union has never relented in its efforts to cultivate
a neurotic peace without security. From time to time a
new offer is made; a well-oiled propaganda machine
paints the sky blue; *Pravda* becomes insipid and even
more dull; and the Russian ballet goes on tour. This may

sound facetious. But the fact remains that this sort of Soviet overture is not a genuine offer of coexistence, but merely the courteous invitation to surrender. Such offers are nothing other than limited time allowances. Should results not be forthcoming, the series of attritional annoyances can be resumed to quicken the pace of our supposed downfall. Thus the peace offered by Soviet coexistence is a rather hazardous way of life.

Relying on this strategic game the Soviets refuse to remove—and in most cases refuse even to discuss—the genuine causes of tension.

Whenever the winning of their immediate objective is frustrated, the Soviet tactic is to bring about a series of crises verging on, but thus far not exceeding, the brink of war. The Soviets have no compunction about using the tactic of the little "bush" war by proxy, which can be easily directed and localized. This is a problem of conventional warfare carried on by unconventional means; solving it calls for countermeasures which we have not yet adequately developed. And we may not yet have drawn the proper conclusions from our experiences.

The Soviets employ another trick which we still have not really learned to counter. In a highly critical situation they suddenly relax pressure while leaving intact all the conditions that made it a critical situation in the first place. Of course, pressure can then be renewed at will. The people immediately affected by these tactics, as well as their neighbors, are to be drained of their power to resist. If these people can still find the strength to defend their freedom and rights stubbornly, a situation

arises that works like a time bomb. This even the
Kremlin has learned to fear.

The Communist policy of coexistence is a complicated
strategy with many ramifications. However, it is not too
complicated for us to draw sound and reliable judgments
of our opponent when developing a strategy of our own.

Historical comparisons can be misleading; they can
lead to particularly dangerous errors when they are applied to a modern totalitarian state. And yet I think that
a remark by John Quincy Adams is worth recalling in
this connection. When President Monroe and his cabinet
discussed the draft of his annual message to Congress in
November 1823, the President at one point seemed to
doubt whether the political principles which would soon
become the Monroe Doctrine should be couched in such
emphatic republicanism: would this not injure the con-
firmed principles of the British government? It was John
Quincy Adams who provided the classic answer: "My
confidence in cooperation with England does not rest
on her principles, but on her interests."

That strikes me as a trenchant reply, also in application to the problem of coexistence. The doctrinaire
principles adhered to by Communist leaders do influence
their behavior, but these principles also can be altered in
the interests of Soviet power as well as of Soviet society.
One thing seems certain to me: the chance of having
genuine coexistence in our world does depend on the
genuine interests and not on the theoretical principles of
the Soviet Union.

5

What does Khrushchev hope to achieve with his "alternating" coexistence policy? As far as we can comprehend, his main purpose is threefold: (1) to avoid an atomic war; (2) to weaken the Western alliance; and (3) to draw the uncommitted nations into his orbit. On one point his interests coincide with our interests: we both want to prevent a military collision of the nuclear powers. That is the point where leverage can be applied to extend the range of common interests, the point of urgency where all want to see coexistence established on a firmer footing and where agreements for joint action by the rivals are possible—joint actions that could have far broader ramifications than the questions of arms control with which they are directly concerned.

Faced with a situation where the strength achieved by the Soviet Union was offset by a certain balance of nuclear forces, Khrushchev threw overboard the traditional doctrine of the inevitability of wars.

Communist leadership has not abandoned the hope of world supremacy. But even if they do like to add fuel to the flames of crisis, they nevertheless show little inclination to embark upon the suicidal adventure of a *major* war. There remains the risk of a spreading local conflict that could become a world war. It certainly has not become less justifiable to be concerned about that danger.

Faced with the nuclear equilibrium, the Soviet leadership, whether they like it or not, must reconcile themselves to the disagreeable truth that there is one vital interest which they share with the "imperialists," namely, that of preventing the great holocaust. This does not mean that the basic conflict is not still irreconcilable in Communist eyes.

What has happened to Khrushchev's other expectations with respect to coexistence? Instead of the predicted weakening and possible dissolution of Western solidarity, the political unity and economic cooperation of the West is gaining ground in non-Communist Europe. The possibility of a concrete Atlantic partnership is now within our reach. Communist influence has not increased in a single European country where the will of the people is expressed in free elections. On the contrary, it is in the Communist camp itself where signs of a differentiating process have become apparent—indeed, so much so that we can no longer speak of a monolithic Eastern bloc. Peiping has refused to acquiesce to the Kremlin's tutelage either in ideology or in policy; Moscow in turn has condemned Albania for its heresy under China's tutelage. Yugoslavia has not returned to the fold.* Poland has shown a will of her own and has gained a measure of success with her unorthodox domestic policies, especially with an agricultural system which, according to the textbooks, a Communist country should not have.

---

* Someone might question this after Tito's visit to the Soviet Union in December 1962. Yet that really did not signify a "return to the fold."

People within the Soviet orbit will become ever more vocal, more insistent in demanding their human rights. A modern industrial society, whether founded on democratic principles or not, is incompatible with a regime of *total* suppression; such a society creates conditions which require, and also make room for, a certain amount of individual freedom. As an industrial society the Soviet Union cannot evade these inherent pressures. The development of Soviet society since Stalin's death is quite revealing in this respect.

In the developing countries, too, the anticipated great Communist breakthrough has not yet occurred. Russia and China are operating at cross purposes in this field. In India and in Guinea the Communists have lost ground. The overweening presumption of "big brother" has not gained favor in Egypt, in Iraq, or in the Congo. In consequence, the "soft line" vis-à-vis the developing nations has been partially abandoned.

To all this one might reply: "What about Cuba?" This is, of course, a subject better known in the United States than in Europe. However, I would like to express the heretical opinion that Cuba is an example not only of Communist provocation but also of the West's inability to react properly and promptly enough to problems that arise in the wake of social revolutions. This comment, while not very helpful at present, may be worth remembering in this context.*

* The reader will recognize that these remarks do not refer to the Cuban crisis of October 1962 but rather to developments in preceding years.

The youth of the Eastern bloc have become restless. Bureaucratic government is frequently criticized, and the young have ideas about a new humanistic socialism. Thus, within the heart of the Communist system, we are winning new allies in the struggle for freedom.

In a geographic sense, we are not engaged in an East-West conflict at all. The free world is really not identical with the non-Communist world. West of the Iron Curtain there are anti-Communist countries—and for this reason welcome allies—that are not citadels of freedom. Either out of habit or fear they are governed by dictators. On the other hand, a completely unified Communist camp does not exist either. Yet on both sides of the line there does exist a camp of freedom, out of which something like a "second front" may emerge.

The past years have shown that the idea of a mutual effort by nations to define for each other and then respect the interests of each is a concept that the Soviet Union approves only as far as its own interests are affected. The Soviets want to have their part of the cake and eat ours too—or at least they want a share of ours.

Our awareness of the motives prompting Soviet pronouncements on coexistence prevent us from accepting their version, in whole or in part. But we know that we can only prevail today by asserting our rights and, at the same time, our readiness to coexist in the true sense of the word.

The true revolution of our times reaches far beyond the scope of the East-West conflict. It does not en-

courage that blithe self-confidence which so often inspired revolutionaries in former days. Today there is no
room left for naïve optimism. We must base our self-
confidence and our enthusiasm on firmer substance, ma-
terially and morally. Today we must have the capacity
to live with the bomb and to live with an opponent who
also possesses the bomb. We must be able to live with
uncertainty. Like our adversary we must pursue policies
which can limit the risks of the conflict, and yet not for
an instant can we fail to guard our real interests in that
same, decisive conflict. We must not allow ourselves to
be paralyzed, as is the rabbit by the snake. If we are
passive, if we only react to the deeds of an opponent so
confident of victory, we will be worn out, and in the end
we will be crushed.

We must decide what we want, and also what we
think we can achieve. That is what should guide our
actions, and we have to seize the initiative.

6

There are two basic attitudes in the West. On one
side, there are those who still view the Soviet Union as
a major power whose interests can be comprehended in
terms of traditional *Realpolitik*. According to this view,
Soviet policy largely follows the unchanged dictates of
Great Russia's raison d'état and conforms, more or less,
to certain customary rules of the diplomatic game. The
present international conflict, accordingly, is considered
to be essentially the reflection of the rivalry customary
between two superpowers.

If we follow this line of reasoning the present international conflict could either be settled by resorting to war or in some other classical manner. In the latter instance a measure of confidence in the essential fairness of the opponent must be assumed. In careful give and take one might seek to reach a rapprochement, a more or less lasting adjustment of interests, and even an equilibrium of strength. It is part of such a policy that the opponent should not be offered too harsh a challenge. And on occasion, in order to avoid conflict, such a policy may extend the innate readiness to compromise right up to the limits of one's own national interests.

Perhaps there is an element of validity in this view. Much of Soviet policy can indeed be interpreted in the classic terms of great-power politics. Our present situation undoubtedly does bear many of the characteristics of a rivalry between two great powers.

Yet this thesis is insufficient to explain the character of our present conflict. Those who take this more static view are exaggerating—to my mind, at least—the importance of the continuity of Russian history and diplomacy. If there had never been a Bolshevik Revolution in Russia then persistent great-power rivalry would not have assumed the peculiar forms with which we have now become familiar. In the traditional manner of balance-of-power politics, other powers would be shifting their weight about between the poles. It takes a revolution these days before a nation can change sides, especially in the Eastern bloc. Old-fashioned power politics might create a Danzig, but it takes a struggle between ideologies to produce an absurdity like the Berlin Wall.

Those who think of the East-West conflict in the terms of traditional great-power politics give insufficient weight to the fact that since 1917 Russia has been governed by a one-party dictatorship which justifies its totalitarian rule with faith in a messianic mission that takes in the whole world. The Communist leaders are convinced that they are the sole repository of historic truth and that the future will inevitably be theirs.

This then is the other position, which takes seriously the goal the Bolsheviks have set themselves. For it is this goal which makes the conflict irreconcilable. The conflict can only end when the Soviet leadership abandons its purpose or its rule over Russia is ended, or when the whole world has become Communist.

Ideological struggles have a vehemence of their own. That was true of the crusades against Islam and the protracted European controversy which reached its culmination in the Thirty Years' War. In these religious struggles issues of faith mingled with economic interests and power politics. But it was the ideological overtones that made these bitter, tenacious struggles which lasted so long.

It would not be realistic on our part to call for an ideological coexistence which Khrushchev does not want and which we ourselves could only desire in a very limited way. What we can and should seek to do is to create a state of affairs in which ideology will cease playing the dominant role.

In the long run the Communist missionary idea may

lose some of its aggressiveness. Yet, even if that should happen, we cannot expect Communists to repudiate openly the theory of world revolution; this would mean the end of Communism itself. To this day Khrushchev and his followers still believe in total victory. It still determines their methods and is the major motivating force behind their policy. This fact explains the bitterness of the conflict as well as its many variants, which range from traditional diplomacy to worldwide civil war, including every kind of slander, blackmail, propaganda, and economic warfare—in brief, the cold war.

The Soviets ceaselessly attack the position of their enemy. To them, any willingness to compromise in order to achieve a lasting settlement is a sign of weakness. Against such an enemy, one can only maintain one's position if one is prepared, as they are, not only to stand fast, but also to attack the enemy's position with the same intensity and commitment.

What we require is a moral position and methods of a political offensive that are equal to the challenge of these times. Our political strategy must proceed from the realization that coexistence cannot work unless we free ourselves from the lurking suspicion of Communist superiority. We must be free, as well, of that careless unconcern which has its roots in the naïvely optimistic belief that a good cause must automatically triumph simply because it is good.

I have learned in Berlin that we need not be afraid of Communism. As a Berliner, I have also learned that the ideas to which we are committed and the cause which we serve—and for which we are prepared to render personal sacrifices—still possess their inherent fascination. This is especially true today.

I have also learned that there are three situations in which an ideological opponent can become dangerous: when he is an uncontrollably fanatic gambler, when he thinks he already has the victory in his pocket, or when the fear of defeat drives him to a desperate extreme. Our political strategy will have to make provisions for all three contingencies.

Realistic self-confidence does not fall into one's lap. It comes from hard effort, from political, social, and economic effort, and behind the shield of an adequate military effort. If our self-confidence is realistic, if we know that we possess the truer and superior view of man, we should have no cause to fear close and constant contact with the political and ideological opponent. On the contrary, we should seek that kind of contact.

We cannot afford to get too close to this adversary nor dare we put too great a distance between him and ourselves. As Mayor of Berlin I have learned also to feel safer when our adversary is not only in sight but also in close range.

In Germany we have a game similar to Indian wrestling that describes very well what is required here. Two men stand opposite each other, each braced with one foot against the other's, and clasping each other by one hand. Each seeks to throw his rival off balance, by pushing or by pulling. Each feels the rival's slightest pressure and can counter appropriately. Since they have each other by the hand, neither can surprise the other unfairly with a punch or a stab. Sensible contacts between East and West are something like this: a way for each to test the other and to keep the other under a certain control.

The uncertainty of our times imposes a certain political strategy upon us; we must continually prove to the adversary that we are as well prepared as we are determined to defend ourselves. The uncertainty of our times must not make us uncertain or indecisive ourselves. The enemy must be taught to expect from us, in every instance, the fitting answer: equal to any provocation, any incident, any attack.

In my opinion, however, the policy of keeping in close touch with the enemy makes sense only if we also take active advantage of it by keeping up a dialogue with him. To talk means also to negotiate. But a readiness to negotiate does not imply a readiness to make unilateral concessions. Concessions that are not based on a reasonable give and take are nothing but surrender on the installment plan.

The Berliners fully understand that the American policy, based on a sober, cautious appraisal of the facts, is to keep the dialogue on Berlin going, patiently and without illusions. Our joint responsibility for world peace requires that we allow no doubt to arise about our determination not to withdraw one inch from our position on essentials. And yet we must explore every path that can bring us closer to a reasonable aim, even by one small step.

It seems to me that during the past years the political

practice of the West has frequently suffered from an insufficient ability to conduct realistic negotiations. Realism calls for negotiating without fear of losing through a partial compromise, and it calls for negotiating without hope for total success. I have been made aware of this repeatedly in connection with the German question.

I do not know if at any time since the end of World War II the Soviets have been genuinely prepared to agree to an acceptable solution of the German problem, which is of such vital concern to Europe and to world peace. But I regret that this possibility, however remote, was not more actively explored, especially in the years 1952–1955.

For over a year now, we have been confronted in Berlin with the wall of shame, this testimony of a battle lost by the Soviets on the field of peaceful coexistence. The Soviets have waited in vain for the expected consolidation of the German territory they occupy. The standard of living in the Soviet zone is lower than at any time during the last five years. Production curves have plunged. Never before have people dared to criticize the regime so mercilessly, or so openly. Khrushchev can never put his trust in a "peaceful development" under the Ulbricht regime. He could not count on stability in that "state" even if the Wall were twice as high. The people behind the Wall simply cannot forget that they belong to a nation more than three quarters of which is flourishing in freedom.

The Soviets set out to conquer Germany. History will perhaps show that the Wall signified the culmination of

Soviet expansion in Europe, for, viewed in the larger context, it is a sign of weakness. Possibly the Soviets have bitten off more than they can chew in Germany. They have ridden out many storms. With some nations they have managed to reach a bearable sort of accommodation. But to imprison behind barbed wire, death strips, and a Wall one fourth of the people comprising the largest nation in Central Europe dashes to pieces any chance of normalizing relations between the Soviet Union and Germany. It is also the tangible evidence of a defeat, the implications of which reach far beyond Europe.

The recurrent themes Berlin and Germany are not the most comfortable subjects on the agenda of the West. But it would be a fundamental error to forget that these are far more than a minor irritation to Khrushchev. They are his weakest points, an Achilles heel of Soviet policy.

East and West can, at the most, be only temporarily interested in a freezing of their German positions. There should not be a war in Germany or about Germany. And yet whoever believes that the present unnatural situation can ever become permanent will find that this is an illusion.

It follows from this, first, that in regard to the German question—the problem of its division and its right to reunification—it would be very wrong to pursue a policy of sly winks and tacit understandings, as if nothing more is called for than the repetition of certain well-worn slogans. Second, the principles of a peace treaty

with Germany must be expounded and upheld by the
West, for by failing to do this we create the impression, especially among the uncommitted nations, that
Russia is "for peace" and the West does not know its
own mind. Finally, and this applies to Berlin at the
present time, we must recognize realities for what they
are, and we must fight for every inch we can gain,
through practical agreements, to alleviate the suffering
of people who have been separated from us by the Wall.
We should do this and yet, not for a minute, lose sight
of our wider aims, our principles and our rights—and
these include reuniting this dismembered nation in the
heart of Europe.

We should not be too timid to put forward demands
that may appear unrealistic right now. We must advance
them if we want to do justice to the real problems of this
era of sweeping change. We must press for what is right,
even if it exceeds by far present-day possibilities to right
what is wrong. This applies especially to problems of
international security, and it holds true for the scientific
and economic cooperation that is so necessary for com-
bating the hunger and suffering that is being augmented
in vast areas of the world by an as yet untamed population explosion.

There is another aspect of coexistence which I find
difficult to talk about without a certain amount of bitterness: in the field of cultural communication the gap between desires and brutal reality is painfully wide in my
city.

I realize that British and Americans in particular have

had interesting and, at times, encouraging experiences in this area. It is true that cooperation is possible when it is objectively limited; then it is purposeful as well. This applies to the exchange of scientists and other experts, to conventions in various fields, to cultural contacts and meetings, and even to tourism.

We in Berlin do not, of course, wish to remain indefinitely the problem child of world politics. We shall assert ourselves, but we would also like to engage the active interest of people everywhere in the constructive side of our endeavors. If we succeed in making Berlin an international cultural center, we not only will furnish evidence of our vitality, but will also render a positive contribution to coexistence in the best sense.

Cultural communication with the Eastern bloc, if conducted without illusions, can do us no harm; it might conceivably be helpful.

This also applies to economic cooperation with the Communist world. In this field the West needs to work with joint procedures and a common practice. So far these things have been lacking. This is a disadvantage which can be corrected.

We must be able to appraise specific situations and the trend of development in Communist countries realistically and prudently. That means trying to learn as much as possible about present realities in these countries, about the differentiated reality produced by different nations and population groups, their interests, their achievements, their worries and problems.

Here the question arises whether and to what extent

we can encourage and support the opposition within the Communist camp through contacts with people from behind the Iron and the Bamboo Curtains.

It is dangerous to imitate the methods of our ideological enemy. Certain ideas require a consistent method of intended dissemination. A good purpose does not justify dubious means. The right means of propagating our ideas should be objective information on the reality of our lives. We are not afraid to show it to anyone. Of course we are mindful of the fact that not everyone who lives in the West is a representative of Western democracy. On the other hand, most people who live in the Eastern bloc are not doctrinaire Communists.

There is political opposition within the Eastern bloc, but subversive influences from the outside are really not ever the right means for making domestic opposition more effective. There is no single answer to the questions: should we take advantage of the discontent within the enemy camp, and if so, how may that best be accomplished? Here we must simply be guided by our own best interest, and in so doing we have to weigh carefully what bearing our actions will have on the internal conditions in the various Communist countries. That does not, of course, mean that we must abstain from any initiative. Quite the contrary, our strategy must be offensive.

In determining that strategy speculations about how we might influence the Communists should not come first. Western concessions on test-ban inspection in the spring of 1961 may have sharpened Sino-Russian differences; Western firmness on Berlin may have had the same effect. But both policies were right on merit, not because of these chance by-products.

Western political strategy requires that we constantly seize the initiative and develop a permanent offensive. That must be done on as many fronts as possible.

However, only he who is ready and able to give way on something can hold back when that is necessary and useful. Only if we have relations with an enemy can we also put these relations on ice or break them off when that is what the situation calls for.

If we can manage to link the interests of the Eastern bloc, or those of single Communist countries, with our own interests, we will have created an instrument of political action far more effective than any paper protests.

He who lacks the resourcefulness to maintain a policy of permanent offensive will not even be able to hold his own. The dynamism inherent in the Communist system must be matched by a dynamism that will draw sustenance from the wide spectrum of ideas that are peculiarly our own. Only thus can we prevail in the eyes of an enemy who never drops his guard and in the eyes of the uncommitted nations who watch us with skeptical restraint.

Unity in diversity—there lies our strength. What we need for maintaining and expanding our position in the era of coexistence is not a counterideology which would meet Communism on its own terms. What we require in the West is more self-confidence and less self-imposed isolation, less sterility and more flexibility, fewer reflections on the past and more sound planning for the future.

We must cast away from the moorings of outworn traditional methods for the conduct of international policy and decide to engage in purposeful, coordinated interventions in the process of history.

7

To summarize thus far, we have concluded that the Soviet idea of coexistence is unacceptable to us, in whole or in part; however, it does not suffice to say "no." By merely defending ourselves we will not advance our cause.

Today, genuine coexistence is the only alternative to atomic war and universal suicide. Since we intend to secure world peace—indeed, we must win it—we should be the ones to implant the true meaning of coexistence in the consciousness of people everywhere. It is our business to recapture the concept of coexistence from Khrushchev and his propagandists. For coexistence is really a democratic cause which Khrushchev usurped and which he still employs as a cloak for his aggressive policy of perpetuating crisis. We must win it back.

Coexistence in its proper sense is a long-term test of our moral fiber, a political, economic, and military ordeal. The ordeal of coexistence will probably be the toughest trial Western democracy has had to undergo in its history.

For we face a future of uncertainties. We cannot be certain that we will succeed in preventing war. The further diffusion of the thermonuclear power potential not only will make armament controls more urgent, but can also make them more difficult to achieve. We have barely crossed the threshold of a second industrial revolution that can make obsolete these very principles of military strategy which only recently have found acceptance in the Western alliance.

And yet, it will not be sufficient merely to prevent a nuclear disaster and maintain our position intact in the face of Soviet pressures. We must not be hypnotized by a defensive task. Nor can we allow this one to claim our undivided attention. To my mind, the East-West conflict is not the only, nor, in the final analysis, is it even the most important problem to be solved if we really want to win the future. The decisive factors for the future progress of mankind will be the technical and social revolutions which in our days have wrought such deep and apparent changes all over the earth. If we hope to preserve liberty and our cultural heritage, we simply have no choice other than to become revolutionaries in the sense called for by these values and required by the age.

The technological progress which opens unimagined new vistas also confronts us with new perils. The social problems which will result, inevitably, from technological changes as radical as we must expect cannot be mastered with recourse to old formulas or patent remedies. It will no longer be possible for us to deal with such matters as if they were merely domestic problems of our own countries. The uncertain future of this interdependent world compels our assuring that all mankind can benefit from the technological accomplishments of the age.

The newly independent nations in still underdeveloped parts of the world require our assistance. They need not only money, equipment, and expert assistance, important as these may be; it is just as incumbent upon us, by the progressive way we master their problems as well as our own, to give them an example of democracy in action. Our concept of coexistence is therefore not limited to the relationship between the democratic West and the Communist East. It also applies to relations between the rich and the poor nations. We must see genuine coexistence as a global design.

If we allow ourselves to be hypnotized by the East-West conflict, we will sooner or later see the whole world in a distorting mirror.

Western democracy, founded as it is on the ideal of the freedom of the individual and on a pluralistic society, has a good chance not only to prevail but to win the future. We must learn to live with uncertainty and yet not forfeit an iota of that unique capacity for dynamic creativity and enterprise that Western culture does possess. It will be a challenge to our vitality, a trial of our maturity, the test of our solidarity. For we cannot succeed alone, either as individuals or as single nations. We can only do so as partners in a common cause, and we are not as unprepared as the Soviets hope.

Western man is not ill-equipped for an ordeal of uncertainty. The parable about when to plant a tree, in all its varied versions, reveals a capacity for moral equilib-

rium that can be found in all our countries. I myself
favor a version that goes back to a colony of pietists in
Württemberg during the early part of the eighteenth
century. Even in those days it was not uncommon to
expect the end of the world. Certain brethren had given
up working the fields altogether and, expecting the last
judgment, some of the younger men had lost interest in
getting married. When the congregation gathered to discuss it, a simple peasant said: "Brothers, if I am certain
of our Saviour's coming, and if I still have a tree to plant,
then I plant it first. And if there is a hole in the roof, then
I see to it that it is covered."

We have more than technical resources on our side.
We also have the moral fiber, the stamina, to hold our
own through this competitive ordeal and win. The secret
of our strength is the great diversity of sources from
which it is nourished. Of course, a diversity of ideas and
convictions is also a source of tension and conflict, but
such tensions are the most fruitful element in western
culture and a prerequisite of progress in any firmly knit
union.

Outwardly, Communism presents a monolithic front
which seems to some people to be an intellectually and
politically more effective system. In reality, however,
Communism has enshrined itself in an outmoded dogma
which will continue to inhibit the development of
new ideas. The system has become too narrow. The
structure is brittle; any serious crack in it brings the
danger of a collapse. The importance of moral resources
for taking strong political action is something that be-

came apparent to me during unforgettable personal experiences with resistance movements in Norway and Berlin. As the danger increased, as the challenge grew more harsh, I saw the moral strength unfold. This was what enabled people to master a seemingly hopeless situation both in Norway and in Berlin. That experience has given me profound confidence in what the conviction of freedom can accomplish. It makes me certain that we shall bear up well under the test of coexistence and the challenge of our times.

Conscious of such sources of strength, Americans and Europeans must live jointly as an inseparable community of nations in order to transform the thinking and the organization of the Western world. Accomplishing this together would provide us with a better basis and opportunity for convincing our friends in other parts of the world that ours is the right way; the people behind the Iron Curtain would then see that we are equal to the problems the world poses.

The social and technological transformations of our times must be directed into the right channels for freedom's sake. That calls for a high degree of planning to utilize economic and financial resources. It means that self-restraints and international collective interventions in some areas will be indispensable.

No individual, no group, no nation, will find it an easy matter to pay the price for survival and progress. Every group and every nation is inclined to defend its privileges and its supposed sovereignty unimpaired. And, of course, everyone will try to "get off" as cheaply as possible. This may be the natural impulse, but we must all be prepared to make sacrifices for the common cause.

The people of the United States take the lead in this struggle for progress. This is because the United States is the strongest power of the free world. And though it is true that all will share fully and fairly the burden of effort, it is equally true that the United States cannot be spared the responsibility and burden of being *primus inter pares* in the Western community.

Between America and the free Europe, we need no other bond to tie us together than true and equal partnership. If we correctly recognize the potential as well as the limitations of the age, partnership will determine what the future will bring.

There is no guarantee, but there is a very good chance, that Western democracy will stand the test of these perilous times. But in order to prevail, we must work hard, we must work with design, we must fully employ the resources of our age.

It surely is not easy for the Western community, so diversely composed, to agree on a declaration of political convictions that can find consent and practical application by all. But this difficulty should not deter us from trying to work one out. Let me contribute by declaring my personal convictions.

I believe that the idea of freedom is indestructible, I believe that it is invincible. But I also believe that this revolutionary era calls upon us to search for new forms, new institutions and ties, in order to preserve the life and vitality of freedom and democracy.

I believe that it is desirable and necessary to free men and nations from tutelage and dependence, and then to assist them. But I do not believe that we have the right to coerce them into happiness as we conceive it.

I believe that it is right and necessary to heed and assist all people who wish to subscribe to our way of life. But I do not believe that we ought to despise those who, by their own volition, have decided to choose another way of life.

I do not want to force anyone to his knees. Nor will I let anyone force me to kneel.

I believe that he who espouses coexistence must, by the same token, refrain from any attempt to compel others, by open aggression or by subterfuge, to succumb to his will. He must himself limit his demands upon the others. He must keep his word. He must respect human rights and renounce any claim to the subjugation of others.

I believe that the fate of democracy depends upon our ability to see beyond any temporary conflict, and to grasp the transcendent vision of the essential unity of man and of nations. This is a vision which we must constantly guard—or, more accurately, which we must constantly renew.

I HAVE dealt with the fundamental hazards to the free world as they are so deviously contained in the Communist offers of coexistence. Uncertainty has become the burden of our time, and this does not mean only the uncertainty that the Communist challenge provokes.

We must learn to live with uncertainty; that calls for a moral and civic attitude such as this ordeal has produced in Berlin and is producing so impressively in the United States. Learning to handle the ordeal of uncertainty will not put us to sleep or plunge us into doubt. It will make us stronger.

Our self-confidence and our faith will be firmer when we have learned not to lean either on fatalism or on the naïve optimism that only deludes. America has shown strong evidence of this attitude, and, in addition, a genuine will to do something about it. Today we require nothing so much as the example of action with foresight.

I am a citizen of a divided city and a divided country. I share with my fellow Germans the heavy burden of cruel and arbitrarily imposed conditions. As the Mayor of Berlin I might be expected to deal exclusively with the

vexing problems of my city, but it is hardly possible to
disassociate the Berlin question from the larger issues of
the international situation. While it is true that we do
have some problems which can be termed local, it is even
more true that Berlin's fate depends directly on the future determination of East-West relations. If these relations deteriorate, the Berlin situation is aggravated. The
firmer and more honest these relations are, the more
peaceful and stable will our future be.

Recognition of this prompts us in Berlin to view our
problems in a perspective which relates them to the
problems of our country and to the problems of nations
friendly to us all over the free world.

This is a question of the shouldering and sharing of
responsibility in both small and large matters. It is encouraging that in the American press and in expressions
by national leaders of both parties, one finds so much
evidence of willingness on the part of the United States
to assume international responsibility, and thus not evade
the role of the *primus inter pares* in the Western community.

Most encouraging is President Kennedy's 1962 Fourth
of July address which will probably go down in history
as a policy statement comparable to the Monroe Doctrine. Comparable, and yet there is a significant difference: the Monroe Doctrine, which banned European
colonialism from the American continents, was, notwith-
standing its historical importance, basically a defensive
policy. The Kennedy Doctrine points to the future. It
combines the time-honored principle of national inde-

pendence with acceptance of interdependence, meeting
the need for international collaboration with the offer
of active partnership and tangible, worldwide solidarity.
I feel it is incumbent upon Europeans to reciprocate in
kind. Europe's answer should be as positive and forceful
as President Kennedy's avowal.

I can well follow the President's train of thought
when he says that the concrete partnership between the
United States and a united Europe cannot be realized in
a single year. And yet it is important to let the world
know that the Atlantic partnership, and nothing less, is
our constant aim. The world should also know that we,
in Europe, are prepared to strengthen the bonds of
friendship between our two continents—until it becomes
an indestructible bridge, founded on mutual confidence,
resting securely on common ideals.

In this context, we should not forget that Europe is
larger than some people think; she is stronger than some
would like to believe and more virile than many realize.
The Atlantic partnership is *more* than a military alliance.
It is a natural partnership. It should grow, and I hope
it will grow, inevitably and inexorably, regardless of
what a few governments and a few men may believe or
intend.

2

Partnership in the economic sphere, on the continental
and intercontinental level, is the kind of joint enterprise
best suited to our times. On this basis partnership will
develop and grow into a community which will, in

President Kennedy's words, "not look inward only, pre-occupied with its own welfare and advancement"; rather it will "look outward to cooperate with all nations in meeting their common concerns." In his Fourth of July address the President also referred to this partnership as a design for building "a nucleus for the eventual union of all free men—those who are now free and those who are vowing that some day they shall be free."

I subscribe to these views. And I propose the following points for the agenda of Western policy: (1) the widening of the European Economic Community to the full extent of present possibilities; (2) as the logical next step, the creation of a closely knit partnership between America and Europe; (3) a program for guaranteeing purposeful cooperation among the greatest possible number of non-Communist nations; (4) a careful approach to testing out areas of economic cooperation that reach beyond the Iron Curtain.

The success of the Common Market on the European continent, the probability that Britain and other nations will join the Market, and the preparations already in progress for intensifying economic exchange with America have already altered the map of the world.

The European Economic Community has made startling progress. The steeply rising production figures, coupled with mounting exports, are most encouraging indeed. There is no cause, however, to rest on our laurels. The trials confronting the Common Market are by no means over. One remarkable aspect of the growth of the Common Market is the fact that economies laboring under the greatest difficulties have been advancing the most. In the last few years West Germany has ceased to be alone in experiencing a phenomenal rate of growth. Indeed, the Federal Republic was surprised by the spirited growth which some other Community nations have shown.

In my part of Germany we have recently surprised ourselves. I need not emphasize how difficult it was for West Berlin—a German outpost, as it were, of the European Economic Community—to develop its economic potential. The Berlin crisis precipitated by Khrushchev in November 1958 has been the salient fact of our lives for four years; and during these years we have stepped up our production by roughly 50 percent. Since the end of the blockade and the airlift in 1949 our production index has increased sixfold. Of course we still have our problems. But what many people do not realize is that, despite all difficulties, ours has become the largest industrial city between Paris and Moscow. Nothing, and no one, could have dissuaded us from carrying out our plans for enlarging the role of Berlin as an industrial center and as a cultural crossroad.

In Europe we face the problem of expanding the Common Market. Great Britain is negotiating the terms of its membership, and Denmark, Norway, and Ireland also wish to do so. Sweden, Austria, and Switzerland are seeking to associate themselves with the Community nations, while preserving their special political status.

Let me be quite clear on this point: not only am I strongly in favor of other countries, especially Britain, joining the Community, but I would consider it disastrous if they did not. Perhaps the Mayor of Berlin has a somewhat sharpened appreciation of what the division of Europe really means; I, for one, could not possibly countenance a second division of Europe this side of the Iron Curtain, and this time by our own free will and responsibility. We must not ignore the unmistakable trend of history.

The burial of the old enmity between France and Germany is a historical event. For the new friendship is anchored in the hearts of the people, above all in the younger generation. All who have helped to bring this about must feel a glow of satisfaction.

Yet Germany and France together are not Europe. Nor are the six nations of the EEC all of free Europe.

Understandably it is not a simple matter for Britain to throw in her lot with continental Europe; we are aware of the inhibitions which have been aired with such frankness at the 1962 Commonwealth Conference in London. Yet I should like to express the earnest hope that a way may be found to solve the specific problems worrying the various Commonwealth countries.

Europe and America should realize that we have a vested interest in preserving the Commonwealth's stabilizing influence in world politics. After all, the Commonwealth has produced a mutually advantageous division of labor between its members, a helpful measure of economic integration which offers a real opportunity to those members which are developing nations. Their opportunity must not be nullified by Britain's entry into the Community.

What are required, therefore, are interim provisions for the necessary structural change which will enable Britain to take her proper place in the European community of nations. That this should be so is the ardent desire of the great majority in my country, and of the younger generation throughout Europe. That it *not* be so is the Kremlin's desire.

It would be a real tragedy—and in this context I am also concerned about the Scandinavian and other small nations—if one of the rare opportunities we have been offered in this worldwide struggle were to be dissipated by parochial self-interest and by outmoded thinking.

At any rate, we must not lose patience for the wrong reasons. Divergent economic interests must somehow be brought into a unifying framework. This takes time— even when all concerned are acting in good faith. It took more than one year to reach the point where the treaty of Rome became possible. We cannot deny that the widening of the European Economic Community will pose new problems, some of which will not be easy to solve. If this is true of economic union, how much more applicable will it be for the political union of free Europe.

Yet these are the problems we must solve. It is not only a matter of intensifying the economic dynamism of free Europe; we also should be anxious to strengthen the democratic impulse of the European Community by an infusion of British and Scandinavian traditions. The question of the association of the neutrals—Sweden, Austria, and Switzerland—cannot be reduced to an issue of customs duties and, even less, of perpetuating protectionist tendencies. Here we have an opportunity to test how separate economies can be so geared to one another that they become parts of a larger whole; here the idea of concrete partnership is put to a test.

3

After negotiations between the United Kingdom and the Six have culminated in enlarging EEC, even more complicated economic negotiations will follow between the United States and the Common Market. Yet I do not anticipate that any fundamental difficulties will arise here. Experience proves that such conflicts of interest can be ironed out where there is a reasonable measure of good will on all sides.

There are other problems of economic coordination that call for the framing of joint institutions, and which require even greater skill and foresight. Apart from the coordinated trade policy which is scheduled to take effect in the Common Market after an interim period, economic integration will also require an effort toward achieving joint currency management.

This problem is an urgent one. It stems from the interdependence between the economic rates of growth in individual countries, and the amounts these countries spend for development aid and for defense. The present currency system has a tendency to create special difficulties for those countries whose rate of economic growth is faster or whose expenditures for defense and foreign aid are significantly greater than those of other leading industrial nations. Such a country's balance of payments is in constant danger of showing a negative balance toward its less committed partners. This can have a strongly deterring effect on future willingness to vote additional funds for development aid and for military defense.

For the European Economic Community and for Atlantic partnership, too, our first principle must be to guarantee maximum operation of our productive capacity. Our common interest requires that the rate of economic growth and the credits allotted for foreign aid reach the highest peak permitted by the productive capacity of each country. The present balance-of-payments mechanism works to the disadvantage of our common interest. In consequence the "majestic fleet" of highly developed Western economies moves like a convoy whose speed is set by the slowest ship.

Of course, an understanding attitude on the part of central banking institutions in each country can still reduce the risk of a serious failure of confidence when acute difficulties do arise for one or the other important currency. Such interventions have been quite successful on more than one occasion in the past few years. But that is not enough to eliminate the ill effect of such unnecessary retarding influences in the long run.

This can now only be accomplished by replacing or enlarging the present international practice of occasional coordination; we need an organization for common currency and credit policy, established on the principles of joint responsibility for economic growth and of sharing sensibly the burdens that arise from aid to developing countries—and from defense. Such an organization would have to transcend the European Economic Community; on this all thoughtful observers are agreed.

I am not a specialist and will therefore not even attempt to spell out the advantages and disadvantages of this or that form of organization. But I imagine that it would be worthwhile to start out by considering plans already worked out in the Organization for Economic Cooperation and Development.

I believe a solution of this problem to be urgently necessary for the Western world's future economic growth, and its ability to aid the developing nations. It would mean better coordination of our aid programs through the OECD and other appropriate organizations. That is even more urgent than a forced development of common political institutions in Europe.

Yet, while accomplishing this task we should not forget to form, step by step, the political union of the 240 million Europeans who live on the free side of a demarcation line which the Communists have drawn. I do not favor trying to accomplish everything at once, however. Every specific step toward the practical integration of Europe strikes me as being more important than high-sounding declarations about the United States of Europe. Our American friends should not be misled by perfectionist formulas; one simply cannot overlook the weight of historical tradition that Europe still carries on its back.

Under the leadership of Jean Monnet and supported by authoritative nongovernment forces, the Committee for the United States of Europe has put the question of active partnership with the United States on its agenda. However, it has also conceded that it is not yet possible to create the same supranational institutions for foreign policy that already exist in the economic field. Here we shall make progress only if we are tactful and sufficiently patient, and if we firmly persevere in our purpose to go forward together. Above all, we must have the will to do this.

Fortunately, the Constitution of the Federal Republic of Germany allows for the transfer of national sovereignty, by simple parliamentary majority, to international institutions. And Britain, France, Italy, and the Netherlands can lay the groundwork for such a transfer of sovereignty by taking relatively simple legislative action. Some other countries, for example Denmark and Norway, must undertake more complicated procedures to do so.

We shall have to face more difficult problems than these. Yet, as the record shows, the new reality of the European Community is now an accomplished fact, an indelible landmark on the political landscape. Since nothing succeeds like success, it may not be immodest to suggest that the European Economic Community will become the model for other regional systems. Already we are confronted with the important problem of linking the Common Market with the associated African nations; doing so may be only a first step that should indicate future trends.

Any discrimination against the developing countries must be painstakingly avoided when we plan the future shape of the European Economic Community and the principles underlying its trade policies, and, most particularly, when we set our tariffs. The new nations want to substitute trade for aid; we must not frustrate this understandable desire.

The creation of the new industrial giant in Europe must not even appear to impair the industrialization of the developing countries. On the contrary, we should bend every effort toward increasing the flow of our expanding trade beyond the confines of the Common Market and, especially, into the developing areas.

The Communists will try to write off the EEC—and whatever may grow out of it—as a "rich man's club." Our actions alone can and shall prove the contrary. For their part, the Communists seem to be aware that more than propaganda slogans are needed to match the challenge posed by our expanding economic unity.

4

The Communists have reacted nervously to unfolding evidence that the "doomed" and "decaying" West has generated new dynamism. The success of European economic integration has obviously dealt a severe blow to the self-assurance of the Communist ideologists.

In July 1957, when the EEC was born, the Moscow Institute for World Economy and International Relations declared it completely out of the question, (a) that the Community could ever change the nature of European capitalism, and (b) that it would ever lead to a unified economic system.

Five years later, the director of the same institute

declared that in the Common Market a technical and
scientific revolution could be observed which would
"fundamentally renew the industrial structure of capitalism." This was in the summer of 1962, at the Moscow
conference of economic experts from twenty-three
countries; among the Communist states, only China and
Albania were not represented.

For this conference the Moscow Institute prepared
theses containing the sober statement that the Common
Market had become "an economic and political reality."
It also included a comparatively objective recital of
mounting production and export indexes within the Community, and an admission that its rate of industrial
growth was substantially higher than that of the rest
of the non-Communist world. A participant from the
Soviet zone of Germany declared, in a carefully prepared interview, that Western Europe's economic development shows "a series of new characteristics." "In many
respects," he said, "it is something new." Furthermore,
he suggested that it would be wrong to see "only a
political motivation behind the Common Market, and
to disregard the underlying economic process."

Coming, as they do, from within the Communist camp,
these are indeed remarkable statements. The above men-
tioned Moscow theses also refer to "a new phenomenon
in the development of capitalism" and to "causes underlying the scientific-technological change which is apparent in the world today." No less an authority than
Khrushchev is cited as pointing to "an objective tendency towards the internationalization of economic life,"

which the Communist bloc must now take into account.

Other parts of these Moscow theses remind me of the old Communist theoretician who was asked what would happen if it turned out that his theories did not square with reality. He answered blithely: "So much the worse for reality!" They pronounced the Community "a new arena within which the basic contradictions of capitalism are being fought out"; the new organization, they predicted, would necessarily bring about a sharpening of these differences. On one hand, it was argued that EEC was a tool of joint American-European reaction; on the other, the gulf between Western Europe and the United States was supposedly widening. One need hardly add that they also detected here evidence of an "attack upon the workers and peasants." Really new and quite startling, however, was Moscow's espousal of the British Commonwealth's cause in the role of its savior; the United Kingdom came in for a severe drubbing for neglecting Commonwealth ties!

Without trying to be exhaustive, it is worthwhile to sum up, in a few observations, what all this seems to mean:

1) Communist leadership notices that they have lost the initiative in this field, and that they now must react to the *fait accompli* we have brought about.

2) Moscow has been forced to recognize that the European Economic Community is far more successful than the Council for Mutual Economic Assistance for which they had so exerted themselves. As a result, they

are trying to tighten up cooperation within their own economic bloc.

3) They hope to label the Common Market "a new form of collective colonialism"; with this rather awkward attempt to assault our position on the flank, they are trying to keep up the pretense that only Communism upholds the cause of the new nations.

4) A Soviet proposal was advanced for holding a world trade conference, without specifying just what it was hoped such a conference would accomplish.

5) Khrushchev himself declares that it is now no longer solely a question of international economic cooperation between individual states, but also a question of cooperation between the economic groupings set up between individual governments and associated states. In other words, while Communist propaganda abuses the Community, Communist economic experts have gained a healthy respect for it, and their chief would like, under certain circumstances, to come to terms with it. Khrushchev probably has a secondary purpose in so doing, namely, to counteract separatist tendencies in his own camp by arranging direct terms for economic dealings from bloc to bloc.

6) This attempt to make a new reality fit old theories, however, also shows the extent to which the Communists are still imprisoned by their own doctrine. There is no other explanation for the fact that, on the one hand, they are able to note "new characteristics" and "objective trends," while on the other, their definitive analysis of Europe's Common Market can only be summed up with

tired, worn-out slogans—"capitalism," of course, is the scapegoat and EEC itself is disposed of as "a state monopolistic union by the financial oligarchy." Communist thinkers seem to be still incapable of understanding the new elements of our economic system which is in process of ceaseless growth and change; an economic system, I should add, which has long since outgrown the laissez-faire principles of the last century.

The new realities of this world are indeed far more influential than the prophesies of classical revolutionary theorists. This applies to every part of the globe. The Communist bloc, in its monolithic aspects, has certainly been shaken. Not even the Soviet Union is quite the state it was a decade ago, for one cannot deny that there are things happening in Russia today which were unthinkable in 1953. More attention is now given to production of consumer goods; the individual has acquired certain freedoms; the terror has decreased.

Our fundamental opposition to a regime with a one-party system and centralized economic control remains unchanged. But there also remains the possibility of even greater transformations taking place in the Communist world. Even Communist countries are apparently subject to certain rules of development that apply when a state is industrialized and which must be obeyed if the state is not to fall hopelessly behind.

But reflecting on future possibilities does not free us from today's acute duties and worries. We of the democracies, the community of free-world citizens, must take account of this development with an attitude that is free from illusions but also unburdened by narrow mindedness.

5

Our concern today is, above all, the question of peaceful progress by means of economic partnership; yet, this is also a political task of the first order and a political opportunity of vast significance. If we tackle this task decisively, if we seize this advantage, we will be able to bring about a change in those vast areas of the world which are sometimes called "underdeveloped." We would also create new premises favorable to coexistence with the Communist camp.

The prerequisite for such a policy is, of course, making peace last. To maintain the peace requires at the very least that the equilibrium of military forces not be altered to the disadvantage of the West. Were this condition not fulfilled, Berlin would no longer be free. What military actions and precautions are needed to keep that balance intact is not a matter to be dealt with here. However, my own political experience counsels against thinking that it is sufficient to maintain an effective balance of forces. It is quite as important to make it clear to the Soviet Union, beyond any doubt, that we are determined to defend ourselves in case of emergency with all the means at our disposal. Only an inner resolve to take the last risk can protect us from self-destruction. Any Soviet doubt about our resolution could summon up the specter of catastrophe by accident.

In Berlin we have proved that we do love peace. However, should Berlin be attacked, we would not merely defend ourselves, side by side with our Allied friends. We would also not attempt to dissuade our countrymen behind the Wall from revolting to become free. The Soviet government must know that they cannot pocket West Berlin without running the last desperate risk.

I contend that it is precisely the Berlin experience which has demonstrated the probability that wars today do not just "break out" in consequence of uncontrollable incidents. Wars can now occur only as a result of controlled, purposeful decisions.

Where NATO is concerned, it would seem reasonable to develop further the division of labor that already does exist within that framework. In so doing conventional strength should be in proper proportion to the nuclear potential. Within the alliance, leadership can only rest with the United States. No one else can relieve her of this responsibility; indeed, it would be most damaging to the alliance if anyone were to try. It would be helpful, on the other hand, to heighten the spirit of confidence and cooperation, to strengthen the capacity to reach joint decisions and the readiness to share genuinely the burdens of the alliance.

In the alliance structure democratic controls must be exercised on the international level through elected representatives of the people. Today, there is a danger that after control functions have been taken out of the jurisdiction of the national parliaments, these functions will perish instead of being exercised on an international or supranational level.

It should also be pointed out that a nuclear deterrent is not believable where every kind of local conflict is concerned. On the other hand, it would not be convincing either to rely solely on conventional armament in a conflict that is strategically decisive.

Bearing these points in mind, I favor keeping the atomic club closed. If other nations should either possess nuclear weapons or gain control of their use, the precarious equilibrium upon which the peace of the world now rests could be destroyed. Actually, nothing is more dangerous than nuclear political ambition. In this field I do have most serious misgivings about a "diffusion of power." Especially where nuclear weapons are concerned there is a greater advantage in having a concentration of forces at both power poles, in Washington and in Moscow, and in maintaining their special responsibility.

However, we cannot close our eyes to developments that are in a sense automatic. The scientific formulas which unleashed the force of the atom can only remain secret for a time. The day is not far off when additional powers will have the intellectual, material, and technological resources to produce nuclear arms. The time is nearing when the possession of atomic weapons will no longer depend upon the wishes of today's atomic powers.

Thus what we are now in is a race against time be-

tween the dispensing of nuclear know-how and armament control. The West simply must not let itself be
discouraged by the fact that negotiations on disarmament have so far not been very successful. It must not
cease confronting the Soviet Union with serious proposals on armament control.

Our own strength must be fully and readily available
for immediate use in case of emergency. This, too, is a
prerequisite of coexistence. Yet our will to defend ourselves and our readiness to end the armament race on
acceptable terms are only two sides of the same coin.
There must never be the slightest doubt concerning the
good faith of the West.

Yet there would be no sense for any power, however
formidable, to be security-minded if its population did
not want to defend itself. Thus in the last analysis, military decisions—at least about strategy—are merely a
certain kind of political decision.

The conflict, however, will be decided on a different
field of endeavor. Of course, the Western alliance must
be tightened and military cooperation more closely integrated. Yet, although it unfortunately remains extremely vital, military cooperation is not in itself an
instrument of progress; in a political sense it is not offensive. It is necessary that primary emphasis be placed
on shaping economic, cultural, and scientific cooperation; for the better such cooperation becomes, the better
our competitive position will be in all vital areas of the
great conflict. Futile skirmishing in the economic field
and petty political jealousies between Europe and Amer-

ica, or between other portions of the Western community, would, if they continued, prove fatal to the military alliance.

6

Let us now turn to certain questions which transcend the problems of cooperation in the West.

There is, for example, the Communist proposal for an international trade conference. Without doubt, this is a new device designed to upset the progress of European integration and of the Atlantic partnership. One must bear that in mind. Yet, in my opinion, we should not persist in a purely negative attitude. We cannot simply overlook the fact that many uncommitted nations do support the proposal to hold such a conference within the framework of the United Nations—as did most impressively, in July 1962, the Cairo Conference on Economic Development which thirty-six countries attended.

The Cairo conference called for conducting international trade on a basis of full equality and nondiscrimination. Second, it declared itself opposed to regional groupings which, by restrictive or protectionist measures, would infringe upon the interests of developing countries. And third, it called for a joint effort on the national and international levels in order to step up the pace of development aid, and to explore methods of financing through United Nations channels.

It is not clear to me what these countries imagine they can achieve from the first two points of this agenda. For the genuine interests of the developing countries—in securing expanding markets for their products and protection for their new industrial plants—can hardly be served by universal free trade.

It is clear that the Soviets intend their international trade conference as a protest against the Common Market. For Communists are eager to make the Common Market the bête noire of the developing nations. The Common Market, they contend, is simply economic colonialism in disguise; it aims to perpetuate the dependence of the producers of the raw materials upon the industrially advanced nations.

This interpretation is false and it must be repudiated. It is not the Common Market and not the unity of the Western world that is preventing the developing countries from making progress. We must plead the cause of the Common Market and of the Atlantic partnership and we must explain patiently and consistently what they really mean. However, we are also under an obligation to show the developing countries a way to move ahead through cooperation with us.

We cannot deny that there are indeed important questions of international trade, both general and specific, which must be dealt with. If, therefore, the Soviets or the developing nations propose a conference on international trade, we should not answer with a blunt rejection. In my view, we should take up the suggestion and concentrate our attention on determining a more effective and beneficial agenda for this kind of conference.*

* On December 8, 1962, the General Assembly of the United Nations decided that an International Trade Conference would take place early in 1964.

This is one of those questions of method which should not be taken too lightly. I have been personally concerned with another example: after the Vienna meeting between President Kennedy and Chairman Khrushchev last year, I proposed that we take advantage of the Soviet suggestion for a peace conference on Germany. I did not think that doing so would quickly solve my country's problem, but I did believe, as I do now believe, that the West could thus have regained the initiative. It would have made clear before the whole world that the great majority of the nations formerly allied against Germany do favor a peace settlement based upon the principle of self-determination. Perhaps such an initiative would also have reversed the trend which, at times, has so unwisely led to an isolated consideration of the Berlin problem.

In dealing with international questions, however, we must take account of what role the United Nations could or should play under the circumstances. Developing countries often tend to expect too much from the United Nations, whereas the prevailing attitude toward the U.N. in certain other countries is, at best, only one of benevolent skepticism.

Neither attitude does justice to the significance of this great organization. At present no world body could conceivably exercise sovereign rights both over East and West. We know perfectly well that there is no such authority which the Soviet Union would submit to. Work on plans for a secure international order based on law must continue, but we should realize that these efforts cannot come to fruition in the near future.

And yet, even today, the United Nations is far more significant than the League of Nations ever was. If it has not become as effective as optimists once hoped, it has certainly become far more effective than pessimists once predicted. The United Nations is a forum for discussion within which world opinion is shaped. It is, furthermore, a place where important conversations can be conducted and contacts maintained without the obviousness and the cumbersome formalities of state visits and official international negotiations. That is important. I recall that the Berlin blockade was lifted as a result of contacts which were first broached informally in the U.N. But the United Nations has localized other conflicts as well. The improvised international police force created by the United Nations has proved its worth on several occasions. Explosive situations have been neutralized. Moreover, for all its defects, the U.N. possesses a moral authority which no great power can now afford to overlook.

In short, it is one of the very few devices for bracketing East and West together; and no other organization exists that can assume this function. Hence rather than becoming superfluous the United Nations is becoming more important. If a disarmament agreement between the big powers should finally be reached, this organization could assume far more vital tasks.

The United Nations' present functions, as cited above, are not only important, however, because they form a bracket between what we imperfectly call East and West. This institution also provides the field in which new nations maneuver and experiment. These new na-

tions should not be given the impression—or be allowed
to persist in the notion—that we are interested in them
solely as allies in the cold war. We must make it tangibly
apparent to them that we are concerned with their problems for their own sake.

This means, for example, making it quite clear to them
that it is really also in our interest that international
prices for raw materials be stabilized. It means that we
must show ourselves willing and able to regulate the
allotments of our agricultural surplus in a manner that
preserves the interests both of the undernourished countries and of nations which depend on exporting agricultural products.

We should not only think and act according to the
precepts that the European Economic Community
should be expanded and that Europe and the Common
Market must enter into a closer partnership with the
United States. Beyond this, we must prepare the way
for a worldwide economic community.

I shall not predict whether it will be the European
Economic Community which expands to become a
worldwide body. I do believe that larger as well as tighter
mergers will come naturally and, in the long run, inevitably, as the continuation of the development which
has already begun.

One way of extending the transcontinental links beyond Western Europe and North America, I propose,
would be to consider the joint currency control authority discussed above as the heart of a worldwide "club"
admitting all countries that are ready to cooperate in the

joint interest of advancing economic growth and trade and raising standards of living. All nations should be able to join this club regardless of whether they are willing or able to undergo closer ties in regional organizations.

Developing countries frequently fear that their opportunities to sell exports to advanced Western nations might be reduced by Western integration. This fear is unfounded. The West European market for many of their products has already grown as a result of the Common Market.

The developing countries have a genuine as well as legitimate interest not in free trade and the absence of regional discrimination, but in stable and expanding markets for their products. At the present stage universal free trade would harm their own infant industries more than it could possibly benefit their exports.

Their real interest requires from us a conscious policy for stabilizing the prices for raw materials and other tropical produce. This leads us to the argument developed previously in favor of mutual coordination of currency and a joint development policy by the advanced countries to benefit the developing countries. A joint economic authority for currency management and for development credit (the core of which already exists in the form of OECD) would be in the best position to take action on stabilizing raw material prices. The developing countries must have a say in determining these policies. That should be made clear by the initiators of the worldwide club at the outset.

Sooner or later the question would be asked whether such a club should, in a given case, also be open to a Communist state. I see no reason of principle why we should not allow Communist states to join an international authority dealing with these worldwide economic problems, provided that they are willing to agree to certain common objectives and operating principles. Indeed it would be best to state this from the beginning.

The most successful of Western economic policy programs, the Marshall Plan, was initiated as an offer of aid for the recovery of the whole of Europe, not only of non-Communist Western Europe. It was Stalin who prevented his satellites from enjoying Marshall Plan benefits.

Of course I am aware that the Soviet bloc, as presently constituted—with its strictly enforced trade controls and its insistence on bilateral clearing—would reject any proposal for common economic and currency organizations because this would threaten its continued existence as a closed system. That need not worry us and certainly not dissuade us from continuing to advance proposals which we consider to be reasonable and right.

The work of promoting the world economy's steady growth, raising aid for the developing countries to a maximum of expenditure and effectiveness, the job of stabilizing prices for these countries' main exports—these tasks should ideally be undertaken by a worldwide club. That club cannot, however, do its work unless its operation is based on some common rules. The rules should be simple ones and they would have to be put forward by the initiators, but the club should be open to all who are willing to abide by these rules. Such a program could offer the concrete and tangible benefits to the developing countries which an ill-defined conference on world trade cannot provide.

We in the West should not be guided by narrowly conceived self-interest, nor ought we to allow fear to be our counselor. We need only remember that all the peoples in this world need hope—the hope for a life with security and well-being. This is the task for our generation. It is not a question of military strategy, of gaining a fleeting advantage through military logistics. We are concerned here with such basic things as the production of consumer goods and the raising of standards of living.

The free nations must conceive a master plan for economic cooperation which lays the foundations for the fullest possible utilization of all their resources for the greater good of mankind. Certainly such cooperation will also enable the economically retarded areas to reap rich rewards.

There is good reason for us to hope that the forces thus set in motion could—more than armaments, more than diplomatic protests—compel the Communist camp to accommodate themselves to an entirely new form of coexistence.

What we are here mainly concerned with is the vision of an *entente économique* which would pull widely divergent elements into a worldwide system; it would be based on provisions designed to attract every nation and

every group of nations; it would make apparent that
those who enter such an entente stand to gain from it,
and emanating from it would be the spirit of cooperation for the greater good of mankind.

This would be the proper plane for testing coexistence
and giving the idea positive meaning. Here we would be
armed with our standard of living and not with the kind
of arms that win fleeting military advantage; here we
would solve the really vital problems of this era which
have been raised by the industrial revolutions and the
population explosion.

The proposal of an open club could prove immensely
attractive to the developing countries; and, I cannot emphasize this often enough, they play a decisive role in
our concept of genuine coexistence.

We must search continually for ways and means to
enable many nations—indeed, as many as possible—to
associate themselves with the Common Market, or the
Atlantic partnership, or at least to cooperate with them
in some fashion. This also calls for our having a clear
policy with regard to the Communist countries. No one
should get the impression that we are only waiting to
spring a trap.

I point to this problem because in Germany we have
neighbors to the East as well as to the West, and trade
within a divided Germany not only affects the vital
interests of Berlin, it also affects the problem people face
in trying to maintain contact with one another in both
parts of the divided country.

As far as trade with the Eastern bloc is concerned, for
our part, we must exclude as far as possible everything

which serves the Communist military potential, or which could be falsified by them to appear as "their" contribution to development aid. Yet, there are other aspects and other possibilities of trading with the East.

I am inclined to agree with the view that the discontent caused by material problems in Communist countries increases the danger of tensions that cannot be controlled, whereas the betterment of material living conditions can enhance the prospects of evolutionary change. Surely there is not anything automatic about this. But I do suggest that it is not in our best interest to perpetuate low living standards in the Communist countries, and even less are we interested in helping the Kremlin tighten its monopoly on foreign trade within its orbit.

Finally, there is this to be considered: in East-West trade the West does possess a lever that can be used to advantage; that not only applies in any given instance where we find it necessary to retaliate to economic or political pressures by the Communists. With coordination, we can apply East-West trade actively and positively. For this the West need "only" lay aside special interests and agree to act in unison. That is one thing Communist governments really do fear. For us, this should be one additional reason finally to consider East-West trade the important instrument it could become, to organize it, and put it to use.

7

Nobody can attempt to draw a picture of the tasks of coexistence in coming years without giving the most serious attention to problems of the developing nations. In these new countries a gigantic revolution is taking place.

The political map of the world has changed more decisively in the past ten years than in all the decades since 1776. And the face of the world is likely to undergo a still greater change in the near future.

Since the birth of Christ the population of the world has grown by roughly two and a half billion. In the few decades that remain in this century, demographers say it will increase by another three and a half billion; thus, the increase will be greater in the next 38 years than it was in the 1962 years behind us. Only gradually will the new industrial age mature sufficiently to inhibit further growth. In the year A.D. 2000 there will probably be more than a billion people in the areas which now comprise the Western world; two and a half billion each will live in what is now the Communist bloc and in the present developing countries. This is indeed a breathtaking prospect.

In many areas of the world hunger and want are still the primary facts of life. The population explosion which we must expect in the coming years—and which will only diminish after the developing countries have become fully developed industrial societies—will make the struggle for food the paramount concern of the greater part of humanity. Today, of course, we have the means to produce sufficient nourishment; there is even evidence that agricultural production could outpace the expected increase in population. Studies conducted by

UNESCO and by a number of noted scientists show that there are enough resources on our planet to sustain a population ten times the size of the present one.

What we are concerned with here is not solely whether our conscience can be at rest so long as there are children anywhere in the world to whom a square meal is an undreamed of luxury, or so long as there are millions living on the edge of starvation. There is also the political question whether we have grasped the fact that our own existence in the Western world also depends upon the future development of the economically retarded countries.

We have no assurance of survival if we merely succeed in averting nuclear catastrophe. Only if in the next thirty or forty years billions of people gain access to the fruits of progress and of modern industrial society will civilization be secure. We know that nature abhors a vacuum, that a vacuum attracts forces which seek to fill it. Categories such as the "white," the "black," or the "yellow" man have no valid meaning in this revolutionary process. It is a new process in the relationship between rich and poor, between those who are fortunate and the hundreds of millions who must leave the cruel but unspoiled "paradise" of primitive existence, to which they never can return.

Even if there were no Communism, humanity would be confronted with a worldwide social explosion. At the same time, we do live in a world in which the man in the Kremlin is named Khrushchev, not John XXIII; and in Peiping Mao is in power, not Confucius.

For some years now the East-West problem has been accompanied and influenced by a North-South problem. The latter may one day be the more dominant of the two. In any case, to the developing countries, the Soviet Union is primarily another industrialized state, very much like the United States of America. The more the Soviet Union boasts of its economic and technical potential, the greater will be the demands upon it by the developing countries.

Relevant here is also the conflict of interest in various developing countries between the Soviet Union on the one hand, and Communist China on the other. This is especially evident in Africa. Yet more important, and closely observed by the developing countries, is the race between China and India.

Red China is without a doubt on the way to becoming an industrial world power. But in the eyes of many new nations this China seems to be largely another developing country, with the unique difference that she is achieving her technological revolution without any Western assistance worth mentioning. The terrible human sacrifice which is brought about by her ruthless way of "storming forward" on her own devices is, perhaps, not as shocking to people who can hardly bear crushing burdens of their own—in countries and cultures which are not yet accustomed to regard every individual human life as an always precious thing.

In this rivalry between the two population giants will be decided which has discovered the answer to the problem of Asia's industrial development—India, oriented toward the example of democracy, or Mao's China.

We should bend every effort toward helping India and we must not be too concerned if the Soviet Union contends with us in aiding India.* Every Soviet investment there is missed somewhere else. I see no reason why the Soviets should not deliver aircraft to India. Everything that assists India against her aggressive competitor Red China is of benefit to us.

In Africa Communism has failed to secure a foothold as an ideology. The Soviets are now seeking to gain influence with the "conventional" methods of power-politics; on the other hand, forsaking hope of early successes, the China of Mao Tse-tung is proceeding by the path of infiltration through cadres which play no decisive roles as yet.

Experience has shown clearly that these countries do not benefit by our simply trying to export private enterprise to them. Rather, we are witnessing in Africa the creation of new, predominantly indigenous combinations of state planning and private initiative—new versions, in fact, of what we have come to call a "mixed economy," whereby, in the absence of private capital owned by the citizens of these countries the emphasis in the first phase of development must inevitably be on planning by the state.

In South America we have watched with interest attempts by the United States to create an Alliance for

* These lectures were held at the beginning of October 1962, and hence before the Chinese-Indian conflict. Today, the Soviet Union is confronted by the ruins of her policy in that part of the world. Events have substantiated the ideas expressed in the lectures. The development appears to be proceeding more rapidly than most observers believed before the Chinese-Indian conflict.

Progress. Sooner or later, Western Europe should also do its share to make a success of these efforts.

In the last few years development aid appropriations by the West exceeded those of the Communist countries tenfold. The problem of raw material prices has reduced the value of this balance. But in the developing countries many people recognize what each side is capable of accomplishing. There is no doubt that these countries will be industrialized; at the same time they need also to expand their agricultural production. It is impossible to raise standards of living in the absence of an industrial base. And if the population explosion is to be brought under control, it is absolutely essential that living standards be raised and educational opportunities broadened. That is the only way to safeguard the developing countries from a cataclysm.

To sum up, there is a pressing need to produce nourishment for those who must still go hungry. It is imperative to close the gap between living standards; it is imperative to help the developing nations find a course of their own.

This state of affairs will have the following consequences. (1) As peaceful competition, coexistence will be put to action and won or lost in these countries. (2) As these countries grow in strength, they will also gain influence and power of their own.

In the year 2000 historians will probably not find that this has been either a Soviet or an American century. We are at the beginning of a new era of world history in the genuine meaning of these words. No one can resuscitate what has forever receded into the past by reviving old slogans—such as the "Third Force."

A new force, however, is represented by these many new nations which, as their power waxes, are not content to be relegated to one camp or the other, and which probably will influence both camps and help to change their character.

8

History does not move along the lines laid down by Communist theorists. Above all, it does not move in a uniform way. The polarization of power between Washington and Moscow does keep the world gasping for breath today, but there is also a growing trend toward the diffusion of power. This trend will continue. Our civilization is based on cooperation, but independent of this necessity, and not at all in contradiction to it, is an undeniable development toward pluralism, toward diversity and multiplicity in forms. New magnetic fields of power are emerging. This makes nonsense of the Communist idea of a monolithic world structure.

I have pointed out that this development harbors explosive dangers, yet it appears immutable. We must face it; there is only one alternative: either to help shape it, or to be overwhelmed by it. Isolationism—any isolationism—has reached the end of the road. "Disengagement" in the genuine sense of the word will be neither spiritually nor psychologically possible for any country.

We have to seek ways to surmount and to permeate the blocs of today. We need as many real points of contact and as much meaningful communication between them as possible. Hitherto I have only discussed economic forms for attaining them. However, the same principle applies in the field of culture.

As I have pointed out above, there is no cause for us to fear exchanging scientists and students, information and ideas, services and facilities. Decisions concerning such exchanges should be based on whether or not the plans are sensible and run in a responsible way. We should welcome projects of this kind that are conducted jointly by East and West. Save for considerations due to Berlin's special situation, I favor just as many contacts and lines of communication to the Communist East as are attainable. This is a program and a posture that can encourage transformation on the other side. This is what I think coexistence calls for if it is to be an active, peaceful, and democratic policy.

Here we should set our sights and concentrate our energies on promoting a development which promises us more than mere survival, which can help us to further a peaceful and yet dynamic transformation. On this level of rivalry we are certainly both more skilled and less vulnerable than our opponent. We really have less to worry about.

Since it has been the dominant issue in international relations, the East-West conflict has gone through various phases. Theories of a "roll back" have alternated with those of containment.

Merely to preserve the existing condition is no solution. A policy of transformation is essential. Real political and ideological walls must be torn down stone by stone but without conflict. We must change the character of the conflict. This is a policy of permeation, a policy of peaceful risk—for risk is involved, since by wanting to transform the conflict we are and must remain open to influence from the other side.

This posture is only possible when we are certain of our own values. In this respect I am optimistic, not the least because of the two following reasons.

1) The standards are set by the West. The Soviet Union has set itself the goal of catching up with and overtaking the West. This means, by implication, that the West, although allegedly "doomed," nevertheless remains the yardstick by which Communists measure their own success. If Communist leaders were really persuaded that their people are marching toward socialism with confidence and conviction, then they would not find it so imperative to proclaim production goals and living standards so obviously based on Western models.

2) For the Soviet Union production will be more important than dogma. Khrushchev's goal today is no longer primarily drawn from Communist teachings but rather from the desire to win the East-West conflict. The standard of living and state of technical progress are considered the real measure of achievement by the Communists themselves. They have thus chosen the very field in which we of the West are strongest. The Soviet citizen has already been brought onto a road leading to ever increasing material consumption, and we know ourselves how painful it is to be forced to back up or slow

down on that highway. But quite as important in the
Soviet Union as price increases and the postponement of
promised tax reductions are, and will continue to be,
the announcements that economic objectives, set to catch
up to and overtake Western standards of living, will not
be adjusted.*

At least the Communists now promise social welfare, but what they have said about the rights of citizens, especially the right to freedom from fear, still
lies under the shadow of uncertainty. Communists do
not even promise freedom of the individual. But in their
own camp they will not be able to prevent people from
either demanding freedom or discussing the rights of
the individual. For this reason, I do not believe that
Communism, as an ideology, is any longer a real menace
to us—unless we should choose to make it so.

We should not allow ourselves to be fooled because
in our own society any loss of freedom cries out for
redress, while freedom itself is taken for granted. It is
no sign of inferiority that our governments do not react
in a "command-fire" fashion, that we citizens are not
ordered about, but simply appealed to. We all know
why we want to live in the free world. Whatever its
weaknesses, our system is stronger and more attractive.
Our great political trump is that large areas of our society
are free of political control or influence. Freedom is
strength.

We have another cause for self-confidence: the trend

* Khrushchev's remarks to the plenum of the Central Committee
on November 19, 1962, verify this development.

from dogma to production—to simplify it in a slogan—
is not confined to the Soviet Union. A parallel development is taking place within the entire Communist bloc.
There we are witnessing signs of a decentralization of
power. Khrushchev can no longer become a Stalin.

Facing this change, we in Western Europe must not
make the dangerous mistake of slipping into a nineteenth
century mode of thinking and try to restore the balance
of power. Neither the French-German rapprochement
or—at a future time—the United States of Europe ought
to be thought of as a Third Force for the balance of
power. The historic assignment is to forge a chain of
free communities in genuine partnership with the United
States, which will secure a better life for people all over
the world.

If this sounds utopian, let us remind ourselves that
things are not standing still in the Communist world
either. In the last few years we have witnessed many
struggles revealing efforts to challenge the omnipotence
of the Kremlin. We have seen only the beginning of this
struggle; it continues.

Besides the tendency toward diffusion of power, a
countertrend can be observed. I mean by this a recon-
centration of power, not in the military sense, but a
phenomenon deriving its growing attraction from the
idea of integration, which entails, to some extent at least,
a pooling of sovereign rights.

Not only the United States but the Soviets too—although to a different degree—are influenced by this
development. While appearing to be economic in char-

acter, it is actually and, in effect, primarily political. We must utilize this development in the direction of economic and political integration and make it the very essence of the kind of coexistence that seeks to do more than merely avoid atomic war.

The great difference in this development which is taking place in both East and West, is the goal. The Communists desire power for the collective. For the West the well-being of the individual remains the frequently not achievable goal.

Let us be constantly aware of this source of our strength. We do not need an anti-ideology, a counter-dogma. What we need is confidence in our own cause, the determination and the will to work hard for it. We must not expect to be pampered by fate.

We cannot be certain that we shall prevail, but we can be certain that we have the strength and the will to do so.

I HAVE referred to Berlin and to Germany repeatedly in the preceding discussion. I would like now to concern myself somewhat more in depth with the German question.

In Europe, Germany is the only area where the boundary separating East and West also divides one single nation. That is why coexistence plays a particularly important role in my country, indeed an almost unique one. In the German situation there do not prevail those "normal" precepts of coexistence which more readily apply when the dividing line between East and West coincides with historical and ethnic frontiers.

Other divided peoples throughout the world have very grave problems of their own, but the political and economic potential of Germany lends special gravity to her problem. The conclusion we draw from this may seem paradoxical. The German problem is really not comparable to other problems of coexistence. Yet it has great importance both for the future development of East-West relationships, and for what coexistence can mean.

It is, of course, quite possible to say that the division

of Germany is a direct result of World War II. More decisive for the present state of affairs in central Europe, however, has been the tension between East and West which followed the war. For many years in Germany, a passionate controversy raged about the best way to achieve the reunification of our country. International developments caused this controversy to fade. That has induced some foreign observers to draw the false conclusion that the German people are not too intensely interested in re-establishing the unity of the German state.

In the Federal Republic one school of thought pressed for German initiative. But those who took this view did not possess executive responsibility in the government and were not in a position to put their ideas to the test. The other school of thought banked its hopes on the expectation of achieving reunification, somewhat automatically, in the course of integrating Western Europe and rearming the Federal Republic. The advocates of this idea did not succeed, either.

Both schools of thought in the Federal Republic have been in agreement for years about what constitute the cardinal principles of German foreign policy. Moreover, their policy declarations also agree that the right of self-determination cannot be sacrificed and that we must never abandon our fellow countrymen who live today under Communist rule.

Perhaps one cannot expect today that there will be a positive international echo, or agreement, when one stresses that German reunification ought not to be considered just another goal of Western policy which the Allies have to agree to, but that it has to be treated as an essential point on the agenda of world politics.

To oppose Soviet demands with a positive conception and goal lies not only in the German interest; it is in the interest of the West, quite generally.

The Soviet demand to "liquidate" what they describe as the "remnants of World War II" calls for a "peace treaty" which amounts to a dismemberment of Germany by decree—with two or, if a "free City of West Berlin" is included, two and a half German states. There is only one way for the West to counter such a demand, and that is to insist that the right of self-determination be granted to the whole German people. No other Western response can be meaningful.

Beyond that, I am afraid that Western statesmen have thus far insufficiently recognized what a political weapon the German question has put into their hands for conducting the East-West contest. In seventeen years the Soviet Union and their local Communist satrap have found it impossible to make German people on the Communist side of the Iron Curtain forget that they are Germans. It is not easy to deprive the people of their awareness that they speak the same language as the great majority of their countrymen do—in freedom. It is not easy for these Germans, in their hearts, to forget members of their own families.

Germany is truly the weakest position in the Soviet sphere. If coexistence means more to us than preserving the status quo, if we see coexistence as a peaceful method of competing, of permeating, and of bringing about change, then coexistence must be put to a really positive test in Germany.

Of course I concede that this lies in the special interest of the German people who have been separated by force. But it is equally in the general interest of the West.

The last thing I wish to imply is that it is up to Germany to feather its own nest as a kind of discordant ally, seeking to gain by exploiting the conflicts of the 1960's and 1970's. It would be folly even to imagine that Germany could do so. It is, in any case, quite probable that in the future national egotism on the part of single members of existing power blocs shall not amount to more, and not accomplish more, than the postponement of things they finally will peevishly accept; the tide of developments determining the second half of this century cannot be turned back.

I certainly do not believe that national conceit or racial arrogance is going to help any nation that has grown smaller on our earth to be able to decide or deter decisive developments. I surely do not believe that we Germans or our "German question" are the factor to tip the scales which weigh the forces of the future. Yet it is wise for all of us to assume that no one can force a people, permanently, to act against its own genuine interest. We may furthermore assume that in our time no one people will be able to put its own national interests above those of the general welfare—for long.

The common interest of humanity is to live in peace, have more freedom, and share a more prosperous life.

The German question is not the single key for understanding the worldwide conflict between East and West. But we may consider it as a kind of touchstone for testing the great powers' ability, and their readiness, to find reasonable solutions to difficult international problems and to show they have an acceptable notion of coexistence. The German question is not the cause of many of the tensions that exist in the world, but it does contribute to these tensions. It is one of their regional consequences which, for those affected, is especially painful.

My fatherland is not a world power; actually it never really was one. However, it can take the dubious credit for having provided the cause, the occasion, and the location for worldwide power groupings—at least in the course of the last generation. Hitler, the man and his mad policies, drove most of the nations on earth to combine forces in a united front. They thus achieved something that may sound like an ancient saga today: for a few brief years Nazi aggression bound Washington and Moscow together on the same side of a vast military conflict.

We all know that this united front survived only briefly the Nazi defeat. The ignominious and just collapse of the Third Reich introduced a radical new phase of international relations between the great powers. Illusions about the prospect of jointly administering the devastated German estate inherited from Hitler soon dissolved in the hard reality of Stalin's policy of power and expansion. Stalin not only wanted to win, he sought conquests. The louder Stalin hammered at the doors of

that portion of Germany which his troops had not occupied, the more the Western allies drew closer to their
former enemy.

Had the peoples of the West not found themselves
grimly challenged by this Communist provocation, neither the Marshall Plan nor NATO, neither the Federal
Republic of Germany nor the European Economic
Community, would have become possible at the time,
or in the form, in which they were created. These things
would not have come about had the peoples of the West
not found themselves, during the past fifteen years, compelled to make joint efforts to prevent the Soviet Union
from expanding beyond a point where the West was
unable or unwilling to tolerate a further extension of
Communist power.

The answer to Soviet pressures was the Western defense community and the beginnings of the integration
of Western Europe, including the Federal Republic. In
the Federal Republic this answer was given jointly by
the major political parties, despite their ardent differences of a former time. This answer, however, has not
been just a defensive response; the Western community
has become a dynamic and creative force.

The Soviet Union set out to conquer and to integrate
into its power bloc as much of the prostrate German
Reich as it could; beyond this the Soviets intended to
exert influence, politically and economically, upon the
German zones occupied by the Western allies. In this
way they hoped to establish a base for leaping into, or at
least for reaching into, Western Europe.

Today the Soviet Union has been compelled to recognize that her way is barred to achieving such goals. After the uprising of June 17, 1953, or at the very latest since the Berlin Wall was erected on August 13, 1961, it must have become distressingly clear to the Soviets how extremely difficult it is for them even to consolidate the German territory they had occupied—especially when they are tied to a politician of Walter Ulbricht's stripe.

Historically speaking, the Berlin Wall is nothing other than a confession of weakness by the East. By erecting the Wall they were forced to admit that the German people are not willing to let their hearts be robbed of their belief in a common homeland. The Wall forces the Soviets to admit that an imported government by coercion provides no platform stable enough for carrying on true political competition and economic coexistence with the free West.

The response of Soviet policy to this could conceivably be a change of course in regard to the German question. But the Soviets have been unable to take that step. Instead, their reaction has been to stress even more emphatically their interest in maintaining, and if possible in formally legalizing, the wretched status quo in central Europe. After the collapse of a political offensive that had lasted fifteen years, they wanted to save what they believed still could be saved, namely the permanence of that occupation zone which they falsely titled the "German Democratic Republic" (GDR).

What role do these circumstances permit a responsible German policy to play today?

2

More than once during recent international discussions about the problem of Germany the thought has been raised that one really cannot do more than regard the division of Germany as one of the more serious of World War II's consequences which, alas, has to be tolerated or respected in all its political, cultural, and economic ramifications.

If the status quo in Germany can help engage the Soviet Union for the preservation of world peace then, some say, it is better to let the Soviets have the status quo that they appear so bitterly to require. For the rest, this planet can go on rotating without German reunification. My people, the Germans, are finally expected to forfeit even their legal right to live together under a single government, if the danger of a nuclear catastrophe can thus be averted.

It is impossible to pass over in silence remarks of this kind, for such ideas are being expressed too often by reputable politicians, writers, and scientists. Above all, one ought not overlook the fact that frequently such statements are used to argue that by accepting the division of Germany we can bring about a liberalization of the so-called "GDR" or even an "Austrian status" for that region.

It is quite true that in the second half of this century we are already witnessing strong competition between international interests and national considerations. It is true that we must weigh all the cares that trouble us and all the risks that threaten us and rate them according to their urgency. Under those circumstances, we Germans have to ask ourselves: can we contribute measurably to maintaining the peace under the standard of genuine coexistence by giving up the goal of reuniting Germany under a single government? I am convinced that the answer to this question is an unequivocal no.

As the Governing Mayor of Berlin I have emphasized on a thousand occasions that the city I represent wants nothing other than to continue its work of construction in peace and in freedom. But it does demand the right of self-determination for itself and for those of our countrymen who cannot speek freely for themselves. No one could be more obviously interested than the Berliners in seeing a genuine relaxation of tensions take place throughout the world.

We love peace, just as the entire German people has learned from the bitter years to love peace. But we Berliners also have learned that moral capitulation simply does not pay. It is precisely because we cannot, and do not, want to forget the painful experiences of a hideous past that we stand firmly by those principles of freedom, law and human dignity to which we have committed ourselves.

In this connection I must here invoke the memory of Ernst Reuter, whose example, as a German politician and as Berlin's Mayor, I feel committed to follow. During the first years of the Berliners' austere and not always very promising struggle for their survival, it was Reuter who proved more convincingly than words, to the entire world, that there are Germans who do value freedom and democracy enough to fight and to suffer for them. It is acting in the spirit of Ernst Reuter to bring human and national interests into harmony.

And if we were to find it impossible to avoid a choice between them, we would certainly have to put human interests before those of the nation. We must struggle for every bit of humaneness and human rights that it is possible to get on the other side of the Berlin Wall and of the death strip that runs through Germany. But we must avoid deluding ourselves with the notion that the Soviet Union would set the territory of the so-called "GDR" free if only it were certain that this territory could then not be united with that of the Federal Republic.

It is a fundamental question whether Soviet policy will recognize, and if so, under what circumstances it will recognize, that the German people cannot permanently be denied the right to self-determination—a right which the Soviets are fond of championing in other parts of the world.

Such recognition would surely need not, in consequence, mean an agreement to the automatic re-establishment of German unity in a single state. Interim settlements are plausible. A development by phases is more likely than a choice between extremes. It is, in any case, essential that the legitimate security interests of all nations concerned be taken into account.

Another basic consideration emanates from experiences since the end of World War II, which clearly show that the division of Germany and the splitting of Berlin do *not* serve enduring peace. Instead, they have been still another source of permanent discord.

To resolve the German question in accord with the right of self-determination and by giving due consideration to all legitimate security claims would serve not only the national interests of the German people. Above all, it would help to secure the peace in Europe and in the world.

There is another basic consideration arising out of the fact that for a long time to come, the desire to come together of people who have been separated against their will is bound to be a predominant consideration influencing the thinking of the German people, and also their endeavors. The younger generation in Germany, not identifying itself with the failings and sins of their fathers and grandfathers, certainly will press for the right of self-determination with less constraint and greater forcefulness than has been done in past years. Nor does this apply only to the younger generation in that part of Germany which is free.

To one third of the German people Hitler is not remembered, he is already a historical figure; today's 30-year-olds were not politically conscious during the Nazi era. Younger people can hardly believe their ears when they hear recordings of his raving speeches. They feel subjectively free of guilt, and objectively they are free of guilt. The future of democracy in Germany will not only depend on preventing a return of the past; it will also depend on democrats succeeding where self-determination, the natural goal of the people, is concerned.

For democracy's sake, democrats in this country can and must never forfeit that objective. It should never become possible for demagogues and the lunatic fringe to seize the banner of German unity as if it were their own cause. I hope that it will always be understood abroad that reunification and democracy belong together, that they must remain two sides of the same coin if democracy and unity are not to be gambled away.

Even if we wanted to, we could not abandon the German right to self-determination. We cannot forfeit something that we do not possess—the right of the people in the other part of our country to decide their own political fate. We can *speak* for those who are still prevented from forming opinions in freedom and expressing them freely. But we cannot *make decisions* for them.

Of course, one can say, the world will go on rotating without the reunification of Germany. Mankind can race to its ruin with a pack of many unsolved problems. However, if a chance of solving the German question does exist—and I am convinced that it does—then it will only come as one element in consolidating world respect for law.

It does not aid the German cause or help to cool feverish world tempers for Germans to threaten, under the guise of a properly fearful warning: "otherwise, we will once again become a dangerous source of international tension." We shall only triumph over the real crisis when we are ourselves both ready and capable of submitting to the dictates of law, without jeopardizing the rights of others, without menacing the peace.

Neither our groans nor our tears move the powers that be on this earth. Solving the German problem by self-determination will become an imperative of politics only when it stands as the consequence of an elementary and universal idea which the overall world development makes of prime importance, and because it really does serve world peace.

Our duty to support reunification stems directly from respect for law. What happens today in the Soviet occupied zone of Germany is contrary to written and unwritten law and against the will of the people who live there. I need not document here with details the well-known record of crimes committed by this so-called "First German Workers' and Peasants' State."

Admittedly, the German question is not a comforting theme. But the world would have genuine cause for anxiety about the Germans if they pliantly acquiesced to conditions behind the Iron Curtain and beyond the Wall. Would it not be an awesome revival of the horrible past if countless crimes could again be committed in Germany, crimes of which other Germans knew without daring to or without being able to oppose them? Many Germans have been made conscious of the fact that they brought guilt upon themselves by their indifference, in former times, to the fate that befell a neighbor. Precisely because we have learned this lesson from our so recent history, we Germans simply cannot make our peace with the arbitrary partition of our country and

callously write off millions of our countrymen. This
question is decisive for the moral well-being of my people as a political community, for their national development in freedom. Nobody should want us in Germany to
practise a kind of political double standard for a second
time in our national life. The just solution of the German
question in the sense of self-determination is no matter
of expediency. It is not something of shifting value
which can be juggled about in the calculations of politicians as they face changing situations. It is a claim one
can never abandon, a requirement for the future.

But what are the prospects of achieving this goal?

3

In order to bring about the desired goal of German
unity, one must first have propitious conditions in both
parts of Germany. Second, there must be agreement
among Germany's neighbors, and above all between the
major powers, to any solution. These conditions do not
exist today. Let us begin with the situation in the Soviet
occupied zone.

Until the year 1949, Soviet leaders and German Communists proceeded on the assumption that they could
extend their influence rather quickly across Germany.
The Soviet Union certainly had more than economic
motives for wanting to do so. But even in this first
planned phase the Communists suffered their first shock.
The only free elections in Germany after the war that
could be held under joint four-power control took place
in Berlin on October 20, 1946, in *all* of Berlin—all four

sectors. These elections showed that the Communists could not achieve a political majority in Germany.

Thereafter in the area under their control Communists began the practice of forming and forcing blocs between the parties. On the all-German level, they demanded parity. The slogan "Germans at One Table," the demand for all-German committees, were based on the principle of parity, which made them specious demands that simply could not be accepted by the free part of Germany.

After two governments had been founded on German soil, the accent soon shifted to political and military questions. On January 30, 1951, came the request of the zone's Prime Minister, Otto Grotewohl, that the West partake in round-table talks. This was followed by the famous Soviet note of March 10, 1952. Whether the Soviets were really serious about talks at that time, or whether this was a mere propaganda maneuver designed to upset cooperative relations between the West and the Federal Republic, we can never know. Controversy on this old point today will moult no feather.

In 1953 the Soviets and the German Communists suffered their second rude shock. The June uprising in East Berlin and in the zone could only be suppressed by the direct intervention of Soviet armor. Since that date one fact has been terribly clear: the division of Germany can only be upheld with the presence of many Soviet divisions; a future unification presupposes either the withdrawal, or the nonintervention, of these same Soviet divisions.

For the German Communists, June 1953 was an unmistakable sign of how alien, isolated, and estranged is their rule in the judgment of the people. Since that time, there have been very few proposals with a "neutralizing" tinge. They continued to speak of reunification, but only in connection with the requirement of "fundamental changes" in the Federal Republic. As early as 1954 they began expressing public doubt that free elections were a necessary step in the reunification process. Ulbricht began a policy of counterideology, that is, he maintained that the only road to German Unity lay in strengthening the "GDR."

The attempt to block the adoption of the Paris Treaties in 1955 was only an intermezzo. The problem of unification was now linked, more strongly than heretofore, with the European security problem. The East linked it emphatically with strengthening the East German regime.

In their terms it was only logical, from 1956 on, for the East to use the thesis of two separate German states, which they claim exist on German territory and which can only come closer to each other by negotiating directly with one another. Ulbricht thus began calling for a German Confederation, which would of course preserve East Germany's own identity and inner structure.

By 1958 Ulbricht's policy was trying to make the "GDR" attractive to its inmates. To catch up with and surpass the standard of living in West Germany was the new propaganda slogan. Naturally, it was hoped that this prospect would dry up the stream of refugees. However, even this thesis was presented with reunification in the background because they still felt compelled to pay lip service to the idea.

But, despite generous doses of direct Soviet credits, it was impossible to consolidate the zone economically, or to check the steady refugee flow. Even the Wall brought no substantial improvement in the situation. The Wall blocked all the safer routes of escape, but it did not better the economic situation at all. No longer is there talk about catching up with, or surpassing, the West German standard of living.

In the year 1962 we were presented with what was called a "National Document" about the "historical task of the GDR." In this document, the division of Germany is no longer looked upon as a national misfortune. People should be content and accept partition as final; in their hearts, they should accept the reality of the "GDR" as their own state, and view as its enemy a second German state called the Federal Republic. German reunification is declared impossible so long as the Federal Republic remains what it is—a free and democratic state.

This means stopping the proclaimed competition with West German living standards and production, as if it had become superfluous. All eyes should now turn and comparisons now be made to East Europe, where the standard of living is even lower than in East Germany. In theory that should make things all very consistent and simple for the regime. But the calculation was made without taking the people into account. To call "national" a document which, in cold fact, is treasonable does not solve the regime's problems. People simply do not want to live in the abstraction called "a socialist state," as if Germany did not really exist.

Ulbricht will never be able to consolidate this "state." In every critical situation he fears the danger of revolution. It is not possible to plan anything in the "GDR" without taking into account the hostile attitude of the population toward this regime and the uncertainty which such an attitude produces.

Since the appearance of the "National Document," there have been fresh interpretations and even certain modifications of the Communists' German policy. But Ulbricht has no prospect of playing the National Communist card. The road taken by Gomulka, extensively linking a Communist regime with the national desires of the people, is a course barred to Walter Ulbricht. For with Germany divided, given the hostility of the people to his regime, national appeals can only inflame the desire of the population to join collectively the larger, freer part of the common fatherland.

Of course, for a transitional period, it is conceivable that a reformed impartial form of government apparatus would prove acceptable. Ulbricht and company cling, however, both politically and ideologically, to the thin threads of an international constellation that has arisen out of East-West tensions. This tension is the staff of their life. Any real *détente* would be a mortal peril for them.

It is not by chance that in every dispute about the party line among German Communists Ulbricht, the most brutal and obvious separatist, has always triumphed. He can do so today not because, but rather in spite of, the fact that he is a Stalinist. And yet the "state" of Walter Ulbricht has no prospects and no real future. His only hope is that his Soviet masters will not forsake their military glacis in the middle of Europe, and that they remain fearful of unpleasant repercussions in East Europe should the Soviet occupied zone of Germany ever be evacuated. But these hopes of the despot need not forever seem justified. There is no natural law decreeing that the situation cannot change.

Meanwhile, the imperatives of our policy in the free part of Germany are to oppose any and all attempts and presumptions seeking to upgrade Ulbricht's quasi-state. At the same time, however, we must constantly re-examine what we can do—and what we can trust ourselves to do—both to lighten the burden of daily life for our fellow countrymen in the Soviet zone, and to keep alive the spirit of community between the people of my divided country.

4

The story of the German Federal Republic is too well known to recount here. And yet how strange it is that, despite obvious differences between things that are really not comparable, there is indeed *one* truly striking parallel with the Soviet zone. In each case we stand before the end of a personal era. The zone is identified with Walter Ulbricht, and no one knows what will follow him. Nobody today can tell what the zone will be like without Ulbricht, what new forces will then become visible and decisive.

As for the Federal Republic, today we do know that the era of Konrad Adenauer is over. Nothing was more indicative of this than the attempt, in the last weeks of 1962, to form a grand coalition of the Christian Democrats and the Social Democrats—even if it did not succeed. Perhaps this was a lost opportunity. But the attempt itself should make an impression on our friends abroad, who often ask us so nervously, "What will happen after Adenauer?"

In the free part of Germany we not only have treaties which we can try to improve; not only a Bundeswehr which we freely criticize; and not only a booming economy that for some time threatened to become the measure for judging all things. No, we have something much more, even if Chancellor Adenauer has not been markedly successful in transferring to his fellow countrymen the trust which the free world has placed in him personally. We do have a relatively alert public opinion. And we have a new political atmosphere that, if by no means perfect, nevertheless is far better than it was at the time of the Weimar Republic.

Surely, the fifth cabinet of the Federal Republic was also a chance to take action relative to the East-West struggle, and to the struggle for the future of Germany. Instead, rather petty, tactical motives dominated the formation of this government.

However, the more important fact is that German public opinion had made itself heard the moment people could not fail to have the impression of a possible abuse of power. The Federal Republic is the custodian of freedom for all Germans. It must watch over and enlarge the precious possessions of liberty and democracy. It must be ever alert that even its worst enemies cannot accuse it of an offense against the principle of government by law. The line separating the present from the abominable Nazi past cannot be drawn sharply enough; unfortunately, it has not always been drawn clearly.

It is just not enough for us Germans to prove to the outside world that we are anti-Communist. We have to make it equally clear that we have finished, forever, with the spirit of Nazism. This should not be difficult. Nazi types do not set the tone on the West German scene; nowhere are they a serious political force. Yet, Bonn officialdom—by being complaisant, by negligence, or by bungling—has all too often given the outside world really unjustified cause to worry about resurgent Nazism. This is bound to hurt Germany's name and good cause abroad.

After all, the Federal Republic has accomplished much more than a merely economic and organizing task. To give but one example, it was also a real accomplishment to integrate millions of refugees and expellees into the warp and woof of society, and to do so in such a way that they became neither an explosive political force, nor the prey of extremist agitators.

This German people is better, more trustworthy, and has more common sense than may often seem. This will become more apparent once the energies of people can be focused more strongly on the social and cultural tasks we share as a nation, and when our energies are joined to achieve solutions of our common tasks.

There must always be a meticulous respect for the law, and, when called for, an even pedantic concern with the well-being of the individual citizen. There must be a ruthless resistance, without regard for rank or person, to any violation of these principles. All of these things are a part of the good name that the Federal Republic must earn if, in turn, it is to ask our friends and allies abroad to commit themselves fully to a just solution of the German national question.

In the free part of Germany we must become a kind of model state, a society worthy of setting an example, with solid legal and economic foundations, a society that is intent on tackling the problems of the future and is inspired by a love of freedom. Sadly, one has to admit that we have not yet really created this kind of good society.

Germany will meet more resistance to her hopes for unity as long as people in other countries, including the Western world, harbor doubts about the real prospects for democratic growth in a reunified German state.

Here one must say a word about the connection between European developments and the German question. During the early political debates that took place in Germany on the question of European integration, one of our first worries was that European cooperation to this end might pile up even more barriers to achieving the national reunification of our country. Today, no one would deny that problems do arise from the progressive integration of each part of Germany into two larger economic blocs that are in opposition to one another.

And yet this need not become a permanent breach. For one cannot and should not exclude the prospect that, in addition to changes in the political constellation, points of common interest may also develop between the European Economic Community and the Soviet bloc.

5

One of the major events of European postwar history has been the reconciliation between France and Germany. In sharp contrast to this have been our relations in Germany to our Eastern neighbor, Poland. Of concern here is the whole broad question of Germany's relationship with the states and people of an Eastern Europe under Communist rule.

It is very difficult to determine how much of Warsaw's extremely critical attitude toward present-day Germany comes from distorted, sensational reporting, and how much of it is based on very genuine Polish concern. For, undeniably, the Poles do have good and sufficient grounds, after the very recent past, to be most sensitive on this score. They find themselves in a very complicated situation. And one must admit that the Federal Republic has not shown itself very adroit in opening up channels of communication with our East European neighbors. This is not solely true in the case of Poland.

There is a point of view that warns against trying to

put relations between the Federal Republic and the East European states on a new basis by tackling the job first at the most sensitive point. However, I am inclined to think that it would be more rewarding to start with the most difficult partner. The same question about the exact nature of the relations we seek is bound to come up very quickly, too, in the case of Hungary, Rumania, Bulgaria, or Czechoslovakia. And there is also the consideration that a certain normalization of German-Polish relations would make it much easier to solve the problem with the other countries in the Eastern bloc.

Naturally, no one should expect instant or even early successes to come out of having established normal relations between the Federal Republic and the countries of Eastern Europe. But the real question facing free Germans is whether, even though there are none but Communist governments in the countries lying between Germany and Russia, we should leave it solely to the Ulbricht regime to speak in the name of Germany. The real question is whether the Federal Republic does not have a legitimate interest in helping to form, if even in a very restricted manner, the picture of Germany that the people of those countries have, and also, by being present in Eastern Europe, to be in a position to form our judgments about developments there on the basis of true observations.

In respect to the nature of these relations, content is much more important than the outer form. Those in power in Warsaw, Budapest, and the other Eastern capitals must be persuaded that to build a solid house one should begin with the foundation and not the roof. The roof of normal relations must rest on a firm structure of economic and cultural exchange. In such matters I believe it could serve a useful purpose for us, having agreed on a common objective, to settle upon the terms for achieving it by a specific time. If we are able to develop normal functional contacts, which are mutually advantageous, then it will be more natural for both parties to agree to the precise form of relationship that is most proper and useful.

It need not be our German ambition to have ambassadors everywhere. Even if this form of representation were to come about in the East European countries, there would still be no reason at all for us to consider it as justification for certain neutral countries to establish diplomatic relations with Ulbricht's regime in East Berlin. The circumstances would be quite different; an international courting of Ulbricht would obviously still be an action contrary to the German interest even if the Federal Republic did have diplomatic representation in Warsaw. Nobody can prevent Bonn from using economic policy, for example, to attend to her proper interests—just as other countries do.

When discussing German relations with Poland one must of course include the issue of the Oder-Neisse line. This question is simply not as easy to answer as well-meaning advisers in other countries sometimes assume. To begin with, it is difficult to see why the Federal Republic should be asked to retreat from the position taken by the victorious powers themselves in 1945 when they declared the final demarcation of this border would be settled by peace treaty. It is also difficult to comprehend why the solemn renunciation of force by the parliament of the Federal Republic should not be accepted at face value. We free Germans will honor this pledge and not employ force to change the present situation. We will never endanger the peace on the Oder and Neisse rivers.

But one should not play the game with marked cards. It makes no sense when advocates of the theory that there are two German states go on to insist that the Federal Republic should recognize the Oder-Neisse line. For according to this theory, the Federal Republic should recognize a frontier between two other states, as though it were our affair to recognize the boundary between Austria and Italy, or Norway and Sweden. It only makes sense for the Federal Republic to discuss this border problem if one starts from the juridical premise of the continuity of a unified German state. Or, at least, if one is prepared to discuss the boundary in connection with a peace settlement that will restore to Germany her national unity.

The present frontier between Germany and Poland was not drawn by Germans or by Poles, nor was it agreed to between them. Much separates our two peoples, and the German record of guilt is a heavy one. Wrongs which people have suffered cannot just be balanced off. All one can do is seek sincerely to make redress. He who gives easy approval to a border in order to disregard the fact that it has been dictated by others is not really trying to improve German-Polish relations.

When genuinely seeking reconciliation and friendship, you do not promise more than you can perform. But what it was possible to accomplish in our relations with France should not forever be impossible in our relationship with Poland. A real border of peace may well call for sacrifice, but it must truly be borne by approval on the part of both nations. This granted, I hope within a relatively short time the border will cease to play a decisive role.

Let me return once more to the theme of European cooperation. It is something that need not always end where the Iron Curtain begins; indeed, it must go further. The integration of Western Europe is a fine thing in itself. But it has the added value that it can serve as an example for the peoples of Eastern Europe, to whom we must always hold open the prospect of cooperation, and never tire of renewing it. That will not only help to make the German problem a less prickly one; it will make peace securer, and can help advance certain transformation processes in Eastern Europe.

6

All too frequently is Germany's relationship to the Soviet Union described, even today, as a relationship to the "fourth occupation power." This nomenclature is false. For the real Germany, the one that is in a position to speak freely, and which is in control of its own affairs, is not occupied by the Soviets. The fact is that the Soviet Union only holds under occupation one part of Germany, that she sponsored there the organization of a

kind of counterstate which could not stand without the
support of Soviet military power. This counterstate has
provided its Soviet creator with a most dubious success.
For it is not viable; its subjects, who yearn to flee, must
literally be held back by a Wall.

Under these conditions, it is indeed one of the most
difficult tasks imaginable to normalize relations between
Germany and the Soviet Union. The Federal Republic
cannot refrain from trying to bring about humane living
conditions in the other part of Germany. It cannot refrain from trying to promote contact between individuals in the two parts of Germany. It cannot let Berlin
down. And it cannot forsake a policy whose goal is the
restoration of a unified German state.

Hence, the Federal Republic cannot refrain from in-
sisting that the Soviet Union must release her grip on that
area which today is called East Germany. Up to the
present, the government of the Soviet Union has found
no reason to give up this military glacis with its centers
of industrial production. One well might ask what could
have ever induced the Soviet Union to withdraw from
this position.

Here I am not concerned with renewing that fruitless
discussion about the price that might be paid. For at present, I feel that there is no price that either we or our
Western allies could possibly pay that would induce
the Soviets to relinquish their grip on the zone. The real
task of German policy, in steady and sincere cooperation with our Western partners, is to create a situation
in which it *would* be to the advantage of the Soviet

Union to grant the German people the right of self-determination.

This reflection can only be called realistic if it assumes the interdependence between the German question and the European as well as the worldwide security problems. But the time may yet come when the figures on the chess board of international security policy will be arranged otherwise than they are today.

If such a change comes to pass, then no one can guarantee that the Soviet Union will not make offers that are really worth discussing. After all, there has already been one phase of parleys during which Soviet diplomats indicated quite clearly to their Western negotiation partners that it is they, the Russians, and only the Russians, who can offer a prospect of German unity.

It does not appear that the West has meanwhile prepared itself for another situation of this kind, since it is unlikely to arise today or tomorrow morning. However, when one considers how very quickly after the Cuban crisis and the outbreak of Chinese-Indian hostilities the world's countenance did change, who then would care to trust to mere chance?

The Soviet Union is a powerful country. That is something that the United States acknowledged by giving a form of moderation to the firmest of measures during the Cuban crisis. The Germans have all the more cause to be conscious of the fact. But Soviet power is no reason for the Germans to relinquish their rights—and it is not only in the Germans' interest that they not do so.

We in Germany have our contribution to make to a development in which, one day, the Soviet Union will recognize that it is better to have a treaty-made relationship with 70 million Germans than to have only a handful to trust, a handful who can only pretend to speak for 17 million Germans. One day the Soviet Union will recognize that the Ulbricht regime has been concealing the truth from them, and that it simply is not possible to make Communists of the 17 million Germans in their occupation zone. And that, for this reason, only colonial methods can be used to keep the German people separate and apart.

If the Soviet Union stubbornly clings to this course, if she insists on forcing through a permanent partition of Germany, she is, at a crucial test, exposing and undermining her own formula for the politics of coexistence.

Germany has still a decisive role to play in the arena of coexistence. The question now is, whether the West is ready and able to play a role of her own in this contest.